With love to Geoff for his birthday
May 89. Joan & Allan.

CURIOSITIES of CORNWALL

Michael Williams

BOSSINEY BOOKS

First published in 1983
by Bossiney Books
St. Teath, Bodmin, Cornwall
Designed, typeset and printed in Great Britain by
Penwell Ltd, Parkwood, Callington
Cornwall

ISBN 0 906456 70 3

PLATE ACKNOWLEDGEMENTS

Cover photography Ray Bishop
Pages 9, 17, 23, 24, 37, 40, 43, 47, 49-52, 58, 59, 61-67, 72, 76, 90, 92, 96, 99, 102 Ray Bishop
Pages 19, 62 Ray Bishop by courtesy of Penwith District Council
Pages 6, 53 right, 54, 55, 88 Richard Isbell
Pages 27, 45, 48, 53 left Peter Dryden
Pages 35, 60, 100 Woolf-Greenham Collection
Pages 78, 79, back cover Delabole Quarry
Pages 8, 57, Alice Lennox Boyd
Pages 33, 34 Heather Williams
Page 7 Richard Hawken
Page 5 David Clarke
Page 30 Elizabeth Arden Company
Page 84 Western Morning News
Page 92 By courtesy of Weidenfeld & Nicolson

About the Author — and the Book

A Cornishman, Michael Williams started full time publishing in 1975. With his wife Sonia, he runs Bossiney Books from a cottage and converted barn in North Cornwall — they are literally Cornish cottage publishers, specializing in Westcountry subjects by Westcountry authors.

For ten years they ran the Bossiney House Hotel, just outside Tintagel — hence the name Bossiney Books. Then in 1975 they left the hotel business and moved to St Teath. This is their 84th title.

'Bossiney Books is a little publishing firm much to be admired,' said Tom Salmon on BBC Radio. 'I sometimes think it's the nearest thing we've got to a late twentieth century cottage industry — that's something to be applauded. It takes imagination to be that and not a little courage.'

Here Michael Williams delves into *Curiosities of Cornwall.* Eccentric architecture, strange sporting facts, customs curious and Cornish, Royal too; curious characters and a curiosity that has been driven into invention and innovation; the shepherd girl from Week St Mary and the Hayle girl who made a fortune: these are only some of the sections. Words and a host of fine photographs combine to prove Cornwall has more than her share of curiosities.

Acknowledgements

Authors are usually indebted to other people, and I am especially so on this occasion. My sincere thanks go to all who have helped in providing material, granting access to properties, allowing photographs to be taken and so on. I owe a very special thank you to Jenny Slatter who has been an imaginative and diligent researcher — and who has typed the manuscript. Once more, Terry Knight and Barbara Olds of the Local Studies Library at Redruth have proved helpful allies. Finally, but not least, I am pleased to acknowledge the skills of Brenda Duxbury as editor who has edited this and all our Bossiney titles since 1977.

Curiosities of Cornwall

Cornwall has more than her share of curiosities.

There are curiosities in our Landscape. There are curious customs. There have been curious characters — and probably still are because Cornwall is basically Non-Conformist. It's not quite England either.

According to a *Collins English Dictionary* definition, a curiosity is 'something strange or fascinating'. We talk of a ring or a piece of jewellery as having 'only curiosity value'. We refer to a curious object meaning that it has novelty value. Once more we are reminded of the late Professor Joad's celebrated expression: 'It all depends . . .'

We go into a museum and handle an ancient exhibit, say a limpet crook; to the visitor today that crook is a true curiosity, but to the old fisherman who used it, that object was no more curious than a simple tin opener in a modern kitchen. Time, fashion and neglect all help to establish a curiosity. Our most sophisticated computer of the 1980s will one day become an antique. Our most expensive television set will, at some future date, be dismissed as cheap, primitive and out of date.

I have deliberately chosen to make the word curiosities a wide umbrella for the sake of variety and interest. In the chapter on Cornish inns, for example, I am not implying those hostelries featured are strange or odd, but they do have features or aspects which make them worthy of a place inside these pages. And when later you meet a great inventor, like Sir Humphry Davy, I hope you will agree he deserves to be here on sheer merit. Likewise Thomasine Bonaventure and Anne Jeffries, two very different Cornish women, but both are at the heart of curious stories.

Port Quin: . . . did all the men perish one night?'

'Heights like Roughtor (above) are nurseries for legend and myth.' Cleopatra's Needle (right): '. . . it would be an insensitive character who did not stop and wonder.'

These are only some of the instances — and explanations. I suspect some Cornish housewives may argue the Cornish pasty isn't a curiosity. Nevertheless there are certain curious facts relating to the pasty.

Cornwall is full of wonder. Living and working here is an adventure. You're walking along a cliff path, and suddenly you encounter something like Cleopatra's Needle — it would be an insensitive character who did not stop and wonder. I sometimes wonder, too, as to why and when myth stops and reality begins — or the other way round. Take Port Quin: did all the men in that village perish one night? Now we shall never know and can only speculate. Inland, too, heights like Roughtor and Carn Galver are nurseries for legend and myth.

In our days at Bossiney I remember watching Charlie Bennett, in beret and shirt sleeves, turning slate and stones into a work of art.

Charlie was a hedger as well as a charmer and you could always tell a Charlie Bennett Hedge; it would contain a solitary modern brick.

'Why?' I asked.

'Well,' he replied, adjusting his beret to the correct angle, 'Who knows, somebody in fifty or a hundred years time may stop and ask themselves: "Why did he put a brick there? Was he short of stone?" It's a kind of little joke really. Not a bad thing to make people stop and think . . . is it?'

That was Charlie Bennett, and that's the essential spirit of Cornwall; hopefully some of that quality will be found within these pages.

Some of our Cornish locations also have a curious quality. That chapel on Rame Head may be a strange place for a religious building — some visitors may think. But this small fourteenth-century chapel once housed a light guiding ships and sailors into Plymouth Sound.

The selection here, of course, is highly personal and only representative. As I have travelled across Cornwall, I could have included this or that more. Obviously a publication such as this cannot be exhaustive. To write about *all* the Curiosities of Cornwall, you would need a thousand pages — and you could still omit things which would invite criticism. Furthermore I have generally steered

The Chapel on Rame Head: '. . . a strange place for a religious building.'

Cornwall and Penwith in particular are inhabited by some strange and curious shapes.

clear of subjects I covered in earlier Bossiney titles. The Cheesewring is not here for that reason, or Hurling, or the Knill Monument — and many more.

Personally, I have found exploring these curiosities an absorbing experience, and I hope the pictures and the words will combine to make it a worthwhile journey as you travel from page to page — and place to place.

Curiosities from the Past — at Camelford

To walk through a certain door in North Cornwall can be a curious experience — like stepping back say fifty or a hundred years in Cornish time. That door is the entrance to the North Cornwall Museum in Camelford.

Camelford, some say, is King Arthur's Camelot, and Slaughter Bridge, a mile upstream, was the scene of Arthur's last tragic battle. The whole area is saturated in legend, but this building is firmly rooted in rural history.

Back in the early 1970s, Sally Holden of Delabole, daughter of the local doctor, was a design and communications student at the Polytechnic in Oxford. One day a friend took her along to see her father's museum in Gloucestershire, 'and that started me off. From that day, I knew I wanted a museum of my own. My father helped in that he asked his patients if they had anything old or interesting.' Cornish farmers and cobblers, blacksmiths and quarrymen, housewives and hoarders of all kinds co-operated by either lending or giving items.

Sally Holden was lucky in another sense, in that she acquired this lovely old slate-roofed building at Camelford which once upon a time housed coaches and wagons — horse-drawn vehicles were built here — and opened it as a museum and art gallery in 1974. The spacious rooms with high ceilings make it an ideal setting.

The main sections of the building deal with agriculture, including two wagons and a dog cart, the household, slate and granite quarrying, wheelwright's and blacksmith's tools, cobbling and carpentry. An especially attractive feature is a sensitive reconstruction of the upstairs and downstairs of a Moorland cottage at the turn of the century.

In 1978 Sally Holden was awarded the Pilgrim Trust award for 'the best small museum in England', receiving the £500 cheque at a

The exterior of Sally Holden's Museum and Gallery at Camelford with Roughtor away in the distance: 'I was having tea with someone here in Cornwall,' she told me. 'I was in my last term at the Poly, and was asked "What do you plan to do?" "I want to open a museum," I replied and Lolita, this friend, said " I know the very place." It had previously been an egg-packing station . . . that had moved to Delabole, so it was appropriate that I, a Delabole resident, should come here. It was ideal, the rooms open to the roof, and this platform coming out which made it perfect for Upstairs and Downstairs . . . and the feel of the place . . . as soon as I walked through the door I felt right. The lighting and the walls were all good for an art gallery too. The incredible thing is, though I'd lived here all these years, I'd never really seen the building before coming to buy it. From the road or in a car, you got the impression that it was hiding behind a high wall . . . since then the wall has been lowered.'

Right: Sally Holden and a Camelford neighbour operating an early vacuum cleaner: 'Dilys Philp, a friend who lives near Bodmin, found it in her attic and let me have it in the early days of the museum. It probably dates from about 1903 — the kind that was used in the TV series *Upstairs, Downstairs.* It's called the Daisy Vacuum Cleaner. I've also got a Baby Daisy, a smaller version, but both required two people to operate them . . . not very labour-saving, you could say. It all goes back to a man called Mr Hubert Cecil Booth who invented the vac. Mr Booth saw someone demonstrating a machine which blew dust, and he thought it would be a good idea to invent something that would suck dust instead. So he started by sucking dust through his handkerchief, which gave him the idea of a vacuum cleaner, and much later he added a pump and filter, and patented his invention on 30 August 1901. At first, Mr Booth employed uniformed attendants who operated the vacuum cleaners for clients in their homes. In fashionable society, it became quite the thing to invite people to tea while Mr Booth's employees moved around the guests, demonstrating the vacuum cleaner's skills! It was all a great step forward from the carpet sweeper.' The pitchers, in the background of our photograph, are products of Lakes of Truro, a long established Cornish firm, and the objects on the floor are old cloam ovens.

presentation in London from Audrey Callaghan, wife of the then Labour Prime Minister. The judges explained their decision in these words: 'This museum illustrating the social history of North Cornwall contains a large collection of domestic, craft and agricultural bygones, put together over a period of three years by the present director, Miss Sally Holden, with no grant or official recognition of any kind. If it had not been set up, much of this fascinating material would have been dispersed forever to foreign antique dealers or thrown away. Its creation is an outstanding achievement.'

Thanks to Sally Holden, then, Camelford now has something substantial to offer to the Cornish tourist season: this splendid contrast of a museum and upstairs an art gallery that changes exhibitions roughly every three weeks. The gallery and museum

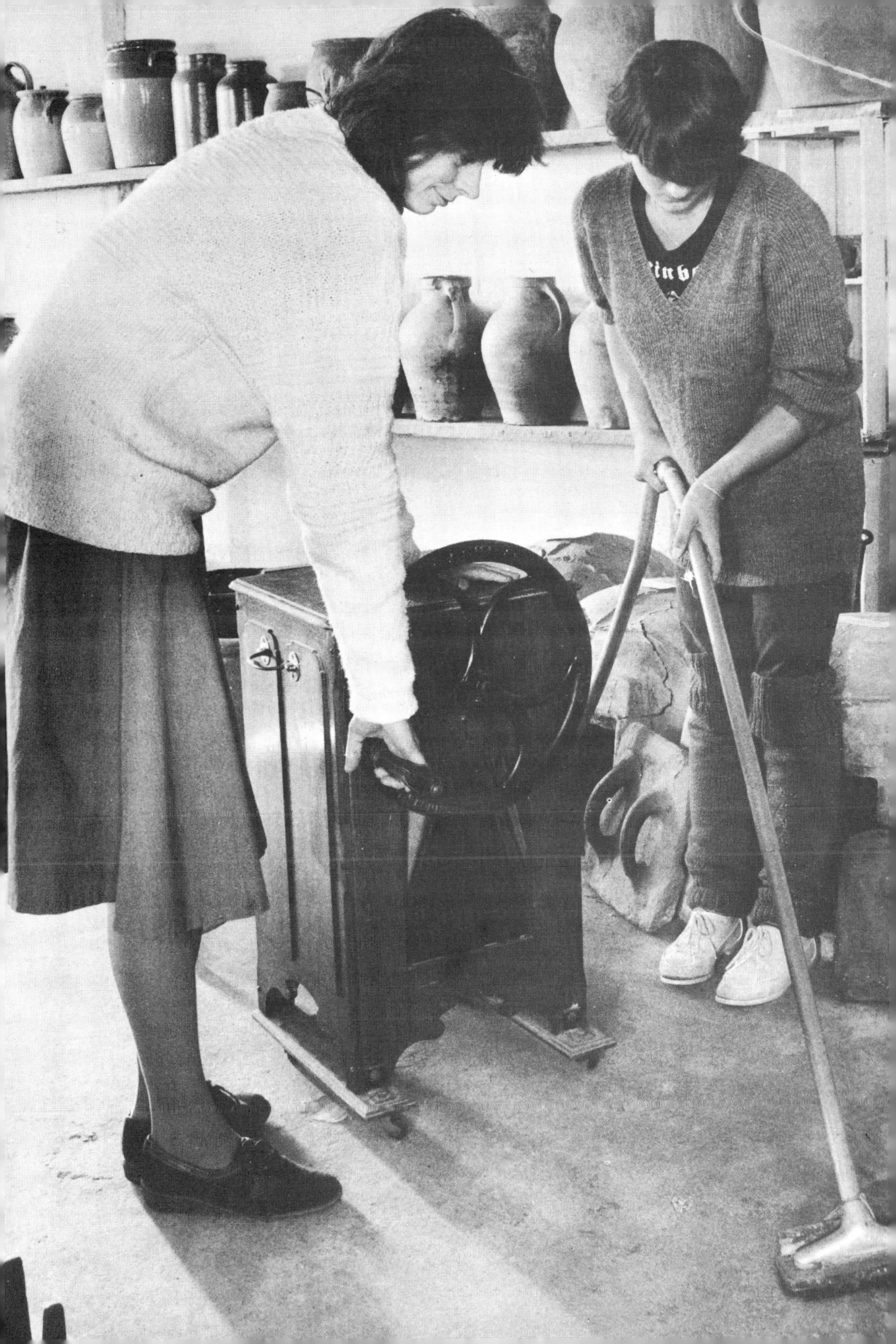

From the horse-drawn days: 'The dog cart on the left,' explained Sally, 'was lent to me by Mr and Mrs Tris Bax of Wadebridge. It was made by Hawkey of Wadebridge sometime in the last century. It was called the dog cart because you put the terriers in the boot or the box to go to the hunt . . . but then you could put the shopping there to. The wagon on the right was thanks to another grateful patient of Dad's: Sam Rush, who lives at Trewalder. He told me they travelled in it to the pub at St Tudy to celebrate the end of the last war. And those baskets standing in the well of the wagon were rescued by a member of the Old Cornwall Society at Wadebridge. They were just about to go up in smoke. They'd been used for carrying coal when coal boats called and unloaded on the Camel at Wadebridge.'

Reconstruction of the Downstairs of a Moorland Cottage at the turn of the century: 'The granite fireplace was typical of many Moorland homes a hundred years ago,' Sally explained. 'Some hawk-eyed visitors may wonder about that birdcage hanging from one of the beams. Well, upstairs a woman has just had a baby, and we've always imagined the husband and the father was a sailor at sea. He'd been abroad and had brought the birdcage back to Cornwall as a present. That's logical because nearly every family had someone who went to sea. Some people think the Cornish were stay-at-homes, but in fact they travelled very extensively as sailors and miners.'

open on the first day of April and remain open — except for Sundays — until the end of September.

Sarah Foot, writing in *The Western Morning News*, summed it up admirably: 'Sally's combination of love and respect for those things in the museum which are no longer used is pleasing. "I like to see the grandparents bringing their grandchildren to see these things, some of which they can remember using themselves," she says. But she also has the excitement of having new artists showing their modern work upstairs in the gallery. So her museum is not just a place to commemorate a bygone age, but also one to celebrate the birth of new work.'

If you are in North Cornwall, the Museum and Gallery are well worth a visit — and it is even worth making a special effort to get to North Cornwall to see it all. A slate pastry board and rolling pin, the blacksmith's fullers and swages like the dark menacing teeth of a dinosaur, an early vacuum cleaner that might have belonged to Heath Robinson, huge fishing baskets from the days when pilchards by the thousand swam off the Cornish coast, a printing press dating from 1836 — these are only some of the curiosities on show. Curiosities, that is, to us, but not to the men and women who used them.

Right: A shoe stitching machine: 'Thanks to two of father's patients, the Vennings of Tintagel, I obtained the loan of this machine and all the shoe lasts,' recalled Sally Holden. 'The lasts were used for making and repairing shoes. They range over all the sizes from very small children's to size 13.' The sight of all this brought memories flooding back for Sonia and myself, because when we lived at Bossiney, Alfie, who operated it, was our local shoe repair man. He ran his shoe business from a wooden shed just off the Tintagel Fore Street. An extraordinary character, Alfie, though badly crippled — he needed a stick to go only a few paces — swam every day of his life at Bossiney. Moreover he insisted that regular swimming helped his mobility. I have seen him in the depths of a North Cornwall winter, smiling cheerfully, telling everyone how great he felt after his morning dip. He died bathing: a way he would have liked to have gone, I'm sure. Recently, I was back in Tintagel and enquired about Alfie's surname. Nobody I asked knew it. As one resident put it: 'He was quite simply Alfie.'

Curiosity & Creativity

Curiosity and creativity must be close relations.

If we look at a great Cornish inventor like Humphry Davy — arguably the greatest Cornishman of them all — we see that curiosity, driven by necessity, is the forerunner of invention, the curiosity probing, seeking new ways.

Market Jew Street in Penzance is one of Cornwall's great thoroughfares. I never come up it without thinking of Davy. He was born here at No. 4 The Terrace in 1778. The Cornish genius is still here — or more accurately his statue: Sir Humphry Davy, right hand clasping *his* miner's lamp, standing in front of that noble Market House which gives Penzance a certain majesty, its dome uniting the climbing skylines.

I have stood in the bar of The Star Inn, just across the road from Davy's statue, and have tried to picture the young Cornishman and his curious boyhood.

The brilliant oratory, which one day was to hold sophisticated London audiences spellbound, found a remarkably early expression. When only a very small boy, Humphry addressed gatherings of children in front of The Star Inn and, when such an audience was not available, he refused to remain silent, lecturing instead a row of empty chairs in his bedroom across the road.

In a notebook, recalling those early days, Davy reflected: 'I was seized with the desire to narrate . . . I gradually began to invent and form stories of my own. Perhaps this passion has produced all my originality. I never loved to imitate but always to invent; this has been the case in all the sciences I have studied.'

His father, Robert Davy, was a woodcarver and gilder, the son of a builder who went to London to improve his woodcarving techniques. I have had the good fortune to see some examples of his craftsmanship: a picture frame at Nancealverne, an oval of twined

Humphry Davy: 'If he had not been the first chemist, he would have been the first poet of his age.'

leaves, and a chimney piece in Ludgvan Rectory.

His mother, Grace, came from a St Just family by the name of Millett. Mother and grandmother were contrasts. Grace was a pious, courageous woman, her mother an altogether more imaginative, more curious character: a woman who loved delving into the past, resurrecting half-forgotten stories about ghosts and ancient customs. It was she who told Humphry his boyhood stories, and from her — in part anyway — he inherited a certain creativity and his love of poetry. Today in an age of specialization, it is remarkable to think that a boy from this relatively modest Cornish background should have achieved an outstanding all-round reputation as philosopher, chemist and poet.

When he was about eight years old, the Davy family, now fatherless, moved to Varfell in the parish of Ludgvan, but Humphry remained in Penzance with Surgeon John Tonkin who, by adoption, became a kind of mixture of godfather and grandfather. His visits to Varfell, though, in these early character-shaping years had a definite influence. We have Anne Treneer's word for it: 'The Marazion marshes, even now, in spite of the railway, have an extraordinary wild beauty. It is felt especially in the winter, towards a still January sunset, when the pale gold rushes are reflected in the water, and the timeless notes of the wild fowl which haunt the pools are heard, together with the sound of their wings. Because of lucky folds in the earth it still seems from Varfell as though only flat fields, and a strange dark wood separate it from the sea and the Mount. The Mount to Davy was a visible symbol of romance; it is nowhere more loyally viewed than from the heights above Ludgvan. On a winter morning, when the sun is low, you may see it in a wash of silver. Davy cared for it most by moonlight — it was under the full moon that he was most strongly to feel visitations, feelings of kinship with nature, which he tried to express with all the resources of his youthful art.'

Typical of most boys, Davy loved fishing — a skill handed down from father and grandfather. He was typical, too, in that he went through the firework phase and later at Varfell he took to shooting and riding. He loved exploring the countryside alone and writing verses. In his new home at Penzance Surgeon Tonkin allowed him to use a garret as a laboratory. One day after a loud explosion, Tonkin declared: 'Humphry is incorrigible! He will surely blow us all up in the air some day!' The boy, however, using an air pump from a

French wreck, forged ahead with his experiments, aided by Robert Dunkin, a Quaker and saddler, who lent him pots and pans from his shop and who in a rough way became Davy's scientific father.

Humphry Davy began his education at the Penzance Writing School. He then attended the Latin School, whose Headmaster, the Reverend J.C. Coryton, was capable of handing out tough punishment. Davy, on one occasion, turned up for school with his ears encased in plaster. 'To prevent mortification,' he explained. Later in life, in a letter, he recalled that he had 'enjoyed much idleness' at Mr Coryton's establishment.

His school career came to an end at the age of fifteen, his last twelve months being spent at the cathedral city, at the old Truro Grammar School, a sixteenth-century foundation and ancestor of the now closed Cathedral School. Truro opened new doors for the young Cornishman: Greek especially and his grounding in Latin was strengthened. Here, too, he was impressed by his Headmaster, the Reverend Cornelius Cardew. But of schools generally he was less impressed: 'Learning is a pleasure; how unfortunate it is then that in most schools it is made a pain . . .'

It was his meeting with Dr Thomas Beddoes of the Royal Pneumatic Institution that really accelerated his progress. It was here at Clifton that Davy discovered laughing gas. He was then twenty, and about this time was painted by James Sharples: a pastel portrait with strands of hair coming almost to the level of his eyebrows, eyes 'tremulous with light'.

These were the days of danger constantly lurking in the mines, fire-damp being the great threat — a naked light could mean instant explosion and death, or worse still, trapped beyond the hope of rescue. Men and boys suffered and died until Davy made his most famous invention.

A small cylindrical oil lamp, covered with another cylinder of wire gauze with a flat gauze top, it prevented gasses passing out at a temperature high enough to ignite an explosive mixture. Somebody suggested that Davy should take out a patent. But his gentlemanly reply was: 'My sole object was to serve humanity . . . more wealth would not increase either my fame or my happiness.'

Apart from all this, Davy rendered outstanding service to scientific agriculture. He helped to change the face of farming. He was made a baronet and became President of the Royal Society, a position he handed over to Faraday, 'my best discovery' as Davy called him. Though a Celt born and bred, who never set foot outside Cornwall until he was nearly twenty Davy was international in that he believed in a free exchange of ideas. Even during the Napoleonic wars, when England and France were locked in bitter conflict, he travelled across Europe with a passport signed by Napoleon himself.

A truly romantic figure, Coleridge said that 'If he had not been the first chemist, he would have been the first poet of his age.' While Wordsworth and Southey both invited him to correct their punctuation and help with revision — confidence indeed.

All comparisons may be odious, but such is Davy's stature that all great Cornishmen will inevitably be measured against him — that, in a sentence, is the measure of the man.

★ ★ ★

For our next inventive Cornishman we go up the North coast of Cornwall.

Whereas Humphry Davy's fame lives on, Sir Goldsworthy Gurney is almost a forgotten man. Yet his achievements were considerable.

He was born at Padstow in 1793, but is better remembered at Bude. Here was another Cornishman whose curiosity drove him to invention — and wealth — wealth that enabled him to build Bude Castle on two acres of land which he leased from Sir Thomas Dyke Acland. A toy-fort-like Castle, it is now the home of the District Council; in Victorian times it must have been a splendid mansion. Although Gurney lived in London for a while from the age of 27, by 1840 he was back in Cornwall, where he continued to be based until his death. Besides Bude Castle he had another residence, known as Reeds, set in seven acres at Poughill.

Trained for medicine, Gurney turned his mind — some would say genius — to other matters, though he did later use his medical knowledge to fight the menace of cholera. He invented the steam blow-pipe and the steam locomotive. His steam locomotive, which appeared before Stephenson's 'Rocket', did the journey from London to Bath — and back — at a speed which amazed many: fifteen miles an hour! But strangely his achievements encountered hostility. Some people did not approve of this man ahead of his time. He was physically attacked on occasions, and his inventive work

Left: Sir Goldsworthy Gurney, 'a Cornishman whose curiosity drove him to invention — and wealth — wealth that enabled him to build Bude Castle (below).

Poughill Church where Gurney is buried, his grave being on the far right, that of his second wife on the left.

was halted by crippling taxes imposed upon him. Those of us who have to pay our road tax and insurance today may have an inkling of how Gurney must have felt.

Disappointed no doubt, but far from defeated, his curiosity turned elsewhere. He created a limelight used in lighthouses, a forerunner of electricity.

The following list of Sir Goldsworthy's patents, eleven in all, tell us something of his versatility:

AD 1825 Jan 11 No. 5068 An improved finger keyed musical instrument.

AD 1825 May 14 No. 5170 An apparatus for propelling carriages on common roads or railways.

AD 1825 Oct 21 No. 5270 Certain improvements in the apparatus for raising or generating steam.

AD 1827 Oct 11 No. 5554 Certain improvements of locomotive engines and the apparatus connected therewith.

AD 1833 Oct 7 No. 6483 Certain improvements in musical instruments.

AD 1839 June 8 No. 8098 Improvements in the apparatus for producing and distributing light (with Frederick Rixon).

AD 1841 March 25 No. 8902 Certain improvements in the production and diffusion of light.

AD 1842 Aug 18 No. 9451 Certain improvements in apparatus for producing, regulating and dispersing light and heat.

AD 1856 June 23 No. 1468 Improvements in warming and moistening air.

AD 1859 July 30 No. 1767 Improvements in electric telegraphic conductors.

AD 1862 June 3 No. 1670 Improvements in apparatus for production and application of artificial light.

He died in 1875. I recently stood in front of his memorial inside Poughill Church, just outside Bude, and read the inscription: 'His Inventions and Discoveries in Steam and Electricity made Communication by Land and by Sea so rapid that it became necessary for all England to keep Uniform Clock time.' I guess he would have liked these words. In one simple sentence, they represent a fair legacy.

The Cornish Pasty

The Cornish pasty can be a feast in itself — a moveable feast at that. But, I fear, many thousands of visitors who come to the Westcountry go away with an inferior impression and possibly indigestion.

No food has been so run down, so badly imitated as the Cornish pasty. The worst disasters tend to be commercial — many shops and cafés failing to ask a realistic price for the real thing. Instead they produce appalling imitations at a modest price. The result is an insult to Cornwall, the Cornish and the pasty.

Historically, the first pasties were cooked in the late 1700s for the lower orders. The march of time and good sense in Cornish kitchens, however, combined to improve the quality, and in its heyday the pasty was a complete meal: meat and vegetables at one end, and apples and clotted cream at the other.

Miners in particular valued the Cornish pasty; though for some strange superstitious reason Cornish fishermen were loth to take a pasty to sea — or saffron cake for that matter. In the mines, there was a strange little tradition in the old days, in that a miner was always supposed to leave a 'corner' of his pasty for the 'knockers', as the evil spirits were called. It must have been a terrible temptation because many of us think the 'corner' is the best bit.

Most Cornish folk insist the Devil has never crossed the Tamar for fear of being put into a Cornish pasty, but one story goes that Old Nick did, in fact, come into Cornwall. He decended on a fishing village, and peering through the door of a cottage he saw a housewife making a conger eel pie. Old Nick was curious and enquired about the contents of the pie. The housewife, summing him up shrewdly, replied: 'You must be the Devil they talk about . . . if you don't depart quickly, I'll put you into the pie!'

The Cornish pasty was an important factor in local industry

'The Cornish pasty can be a feast in itself . . .' A postcard from early this century.

because it was a nourishing and convenient food, so wise employers made sure there was a decent facility available for workers to heat their pasties for their mid-day meal.

Personally I can recall a pasty which seems to have vanished largely from the Cornish scene. I recall my grandmother making what was called — and I have no idea why — a 'windy pasty'. She would take any pastry which remained after making pasties, roll it into a circle, then fold it over and crimp the edges in the same way as a pasty. She would then bake it in the oven, and when it was cooked and still hot, she opened it out and spread either side with jam before refolding it. You could eat it either hot or cold, and unless memory plays a trick, the hot variety was especially splendid.

A.K. Hamilton Jenkin, the Cornish historian, who was an expert on both mining and the Cornish pasty, has a grand tale relating the two in *Cornwall And Its People:*

'The Cornish miner, as may thus be gathered, liked a diet which would, "stand up" to his surroundings. In further proof of which the story is told of a certain man who married a cook who had formerly been in the service of a wealthy family. On going to the mine one day shortly afterwards he took with him a pasty of his wife's making.

' "How did you like your pasty?" was the question asked on his return.

' "Aw, 'a wadn' no good at all," came the disappointing reply, "time I got down fifty fathoms 'a were scat to lembs (broken to fragments). The wans mawther mad wadn' break if they'd 'a faaled to the bottom of the shaft. They *was* paasties, you!" '

Some of the finest pasties I've had the good luck to eat were cooked by Edna Ferrett of Tintagel. Recently I went to see her at her home. 'I'm no expert,' she modestly put it. A lot depends on your pastry, and there are just some times when it doesn't come out as right as you would like. Personally, I use plain flour with a mixture of lard and margarine, and preferably I make the pastry a day or so before I make the pasty. It somehow makes all the difference. A good bit of meat . . . that's essential. . . I don't necessarily say steak, but something of quality that will add gravy and improve the taste of the pasty. . . and you can add kidney because that too improves what I call the gravy quality of the meal. As a family, we like potato and plenty of onion, but that can be an acquired taste. We like plenty of seasoning, but people vary. You can't add too much pepper for my husband Charles, but that might not suit every palate. I cook for the family and I cook as I do because I know *their* taste.

'The Cornish pasty, through so much commercial cooking, has got a very bad name. Of course, some places do sell a good pasty, but I feel in many commercial pasties the quality of the meat just isn't there.

'When I was a girl and we were living at Trenale, father kept a pig, and when the pig was killed we'd have pork pasties, and in those days bits of pork for pasties would be given to all the neighbouring families . . . every family kept a pig — well, almost every family — and they in turn would give other families pork when their pig was killed. So pork pasties kept popping up throughout the year.

'Then there are other pasties. Charles, for example loves a turnip pasty. Also apple pasties, with Cornish cream, they were delicious, but they seem to have gone out of fashion. They were smaller than the meat pasties and you could either have them as afters, or for your tea in the afternoon. It's a pity some of the old ways have disappeared.'

The Hayle Girl who made a Fortune

Hayle is no Cornish beauty, an impression intensified by the loveliness of St Ives across the water, but strangely Hayle is linked to the beauty business and high fashion in a very significant way.

Florence Nightingale Graham was born in Hayle in 1884, the daughter of a local chemist, one of three children. Her family were sufficiently well off to provide her with a reasonable education. As she grew up, she became increasingly interested in her father's work as a chemist, and he, in turn, encouraged her to assist him in the preparation of creams, powder and other forms of make-up for women.

With the turn of the century came a serious decline in the Cornish tin mining industry, a general recession spread across Cornwall. The Graham family, like many others, decided to emigrate, and Mr Graham took up farming in Ontario in Canada. His daughter Florence worked in Canada for a while as a dental secretary, then for a beauty salon in New York. She was an ambitious young lady and wanted to open her own business. With the aid of a loan from her brother, she succeeded in doing just that: she opened her first shop in Fifth Avenue, under the name which was to become world famous Elizabeth Arden. Florence Nightingale chose the names shrewdly: from the titles of two novels popular at the time.

Her business went from strength to strength in a relatively short space of time, and before long Elizabeth Arden was a wealthy woman, inspite of — or perhaps because of — spending vast sums on creating a glossy image through advertising and packaging. Eventually she opened salons in 33 different countries. She was passionately fond of flowers and horses, and became a leader of fashion and a patron of the arts, for which in 1961 she was made a member of the French Legion of Honour.

Elizabeth Arden had that same curiosity, which drove our great

Cornish inventors in the direction of invention. Hers drove her into a pioneering spirit. In the early days make-up was fairly unsophisticated, but as interest grew she led with her revolutionary theory of colour harmony cosmetics which tone with clothes rather than personal colouring.

When the business first started, Miss Arden manufactured her unique preparations by hand, and even in 1922 when a London salon was established in prestigious Old Bond Street, the manufacturing facilities were modestly limited to the top floor. However, as her business grew, so these facilities expanded, and in 1939 the Elizabeth Arden Limited factory was opened at North Acton. By then she controlled some seventeen companies and subsidiaries across the globe, and the famous 'Red Door Salons' were sophisticated fashion features in many major cities.

Elizabeth Arden was industrious, intelligent, dynamic; dedicated to her work to the point of ruthlessness. It is said that on the day of her wedding to Tom Lewis, a bank official, she took an hour off for the ceremony and then returned to the office till late in the evening. This marriage lasted for nineteen years, during which time Tom Lewis worked hard for the company, but when they were eventually divorced he did not receive a penny, because his wife suspected him of infidelities with members of the staff. Her second marriage to Prince Michael Evlanoff, who was seventeen years her junior, lasted only thirteen months.

Before her death in 1966, Elizabeth Arden had amassed a fortune, owned several houses, including a castle in Ireland, had become a successful race-horse owner and was renowned for her lavish entertaining. Modesty, however, was never one of her virtues. In a television interview shortly before she died she said: 'There's only one other Elizabeth like me — and she's a Queen as well!'

Immodest she may have been, but the growth of the world-wide organisation that bears her name and signature is one of the great success stories in twentieth-century business.

From that tiny first salon, the vivacious Hayle-born girl built a glittering empire and acquired a name synonymous with beauty, elegance and innovation.

Cornwall can be justly proud of Florence Nightingale Graham.

◀ **Elizabeth Arden: '. . . she built a glittering empire.'**

A Curious Castle

Cornwall is peopled by some fascinating castles. Perhaps the most curious is Carn Brea — though some may argue it is not really a castle at all — it is a memorable feature of our Cornish Landscape.

The words Carn Brea mean 'rocky hill', at its highest point standing 738 feet above sea level, overlooking the old mining country of Redruth and Camborne. The views from the summit on a diamond sharp day are among some of the most extensive in all Cornwall. Its openness and commanding height made it an ideal hill fort for thousands of years — from roughly 3,000 BC — arrowheads and pieces of Neolithic pottery have been found on the hill.

The castle, on top of the hill, is unusual in that it has been built on a large granite mass which has been incorporated into the structure. Various additions have been made to the original building over the years, the latest being in 1979, when a new south wing was built as a restaurant, using stone from demolished cottages in Redruth.

The origin of the castle is another Cornish mystery — although a building existed here in medieval times. The Basset family built it in the fifteenth century and it was first mentioned in records as long ago as 1379, when the Bishop of Exeter granted William and Margaret Basset a licence to hold services in the chapel. But it became badly neglected and possibly roofless.

The Bassets' fortunes, flourishing from their tin and copper mines in the late 1700s, however, enabled them to repair and improve their curious castle. Around this time it was referred to as a 'pleasure house' — and was used as a hunting lodge or place to be shown off to guests at Tehidy Mansion, the home of the Bassets.

In the late nineteenth century Carn Brea was enlarged and let to tenants, who, under a special agreement, were bound to keep a beacon light burning in one of the windows facing the Bristol Channel. Later tenants, with the growth of tourism, opened the

Carn Brea Castle

castle as a shop and tearooms.

The building is a hotch-potch of architectural styles — much being Victorian — it was restored in the 1930s by E.C. Carvolth, who installed a telephone in every room, but by the late 1940s it had all been wrecked, and in 1948 Mrs Bertha Shelley, related to the famous poet by marriage, admitted defeat by the vandals who continued to damage the place in her absence, advertising the Castle as being 'To Let — Rent Free'.

Having had a variety of tenants and owners, including Wendy Lewis, the young girl who won national fame by walking from John O'Groats to Land's End, Carn Brea Castle was bought in 1973 by Leonard Williams, the Managing Director of a Cornish building company, by whom it has been sympathetically, imaginatively restored -- and has been open as a restaurant since 1980, run by his daughter Heather.

Close by is the Basset Monument. Resembling a candle, this is to Francis Basset, Lord de Dunstanville, a patron of the arts, and a

friend of John Opie, the great Cornish portrait painter. Indeed he was one of the coffin bearers at Opie's funeral in St Paul's Cathedral, where Opie lies alongside Sir Joshua Reynolds of Devon.

Over the years the Carn has been a wonderful playground and picnic area for local people and visitors. The old miners and their families came here, especially on Bank Holidays when Country Fairs, with a variety of stalls, were held. On fine Sunday evenings in the summer months, Carnkie Primitive Chapel brought their harmonium up the slope in a cart and held their service among the boulders near the castle.

Carn Brea then has a special place in the hearts and minds of many Cornish people, and Cornwall owes a special debt to Leonard Williams, builder extraordinary. In addition to his magnificent work here he has, among other things, shaped The Sloop Craft Market at St Ives, once a pilchard-curing cellar, and the award winning Barbican Craft Market at Penzance. His love for Cornwall and things Cornish is summed up in one sentence: 'You can't save everything. . . but it's a pity not to save the best.'

Left: The Castle has been imaginatively restored and is now a restaurant. Below: The Basset Monument.

The Shepherd Girl of Week St Mary

Week St Mary is just a village — almost a small town — it's just Cornish too, standing as it does so close to the Devon-Cornwall border.

In a region that has triggered so much romantic fiction, the story of Thomasine Bonaventure is strange but true, underlining an old theory that fact is often stranger than fiction.

Our true story goes back to 1450 and the reign of King Henry VI. The girl was born in the then hamlet of St Marie Wyke — which later became Week St Mary — and christened Thomasine Bonaventure, a surname signifying good luck and rarely can there have been such an omen.

Although her parents were poor, her father had got together a flock of sheep, and by the time Thomasine had reached her teens, she had become a shepherd girl, watching over them as they grazed on the moor. Wool was a valuable sought-after commodity, and merchants from as far afield as Gloucester, Worcester and London travelled the tracks and paths, buying up fleeces as they went. One day a merchant, John Bunsby of London, came upon Thomasine guarding her father's sheep.

It must have been a strange one-sided conversation between the sophisticated London merchant and the shy Cornish girl, but Thomasine must have made an immediate impact. Initially Mr Bunsby stopped to merely enquire the way, but by the time they had reached the village, John Bunsby had asked Thomasine if she would like to come to London and become his wife's companion.

The Church at Week St Mary: '. . . as long as there is Week St Mary the shepherd girl who went to London will be remembered.' ▶

For two days the Bonaventure parents discussed the proposition. The girl, for her part, was keen to go, John Bunsby promising there would be no heavy work, and insisting his London house was large, clean and God-fearing. Then there was the matter of John Dineham, who lived at Swannacott Farm, and had grown up with the 'milk and cream' complexioned girl. He had hoped that he might one day marry Thomasine. Anyway, a bargain was struck: Thomasine would save every penny she could to put towards the flock of sheep which she and John would one day own.

On a borrowed saddle, the thirteen year-old girl from North Cornwall waved goodbye to her parents and friends. It was the beginning of a story beyond the imagination of many novelists. Their first stop was Lanstephadon — Launceston as we know it today — where fleeces were loaded onto wagons. For Thomasine and her new master, it was a tough two-week journey to the capital.

Mrs Bunsby apparently took to the little girl, and, with growing experience and confidence, Thomasine became a trusted and favourite member of the household. But her mistress, born in the confines of the tightly packed streets of sixteenth-century London, became very 'wasted' and finally 'caught sick and died', leaving Thomasine, then eighteen years old, a beautiful and much admired girl. At the same time, she was somewhat lost, and as there was now no reason for her to remain in London, her thoughts turned to Cornwall — and home.

In medieval England communications moved slowly, but the news of Mrs Bunsby's death filtered down to North Cornwall via the travelling merchants. In the village the news was received with a mixture of sorrow and gladness. It did, at least, mean that Thomasine would now be able to come home.

But before long more momentous news came down to the West-country — that Thomasine had accepted a proposal of marriage from John Bunsby. It got a mixed reception in the village; while poor John Dineham, who had been waiting and praying for Thomasine's return, was so shattered that he vanished. He eventually joined an order called 'The White Monks of St Cleer' and never came back into local society.

Thomasine's marriage lasted just three years. Her husband caught the plague and died, leaving all his considerable wealth to 'my beloved Thomasine', making her a very rich young widow. For Thomasine the streets of London were indeed paved with gold.

But Cornwall still lived vividly in her mind. One of her first bequests was to the Reeve of her Cornish village: ten marks for the building of a bridge over the ford at Green-a-moor, which she must have crossed many times as a little girl with her father's sheep. She also requested a tree by the ford and all the plants and flowers there should be preserved because she had spent so many happy hours by them, and it was under this tree that she was resting when she had that first fateful meeting with John Bunsby. Thomasine, without knowing it, must have been one of the first conservationists.

Her widowhood, however, lasted little more than a year. She was, after all, very rich and very good-looking. Her second husband was Master John Gall of St Lawrence, Milk Street, London, 'A Worshipful Merchant-Adventurer'. This marriage lasted only five years and, even before his death, he bestowed all his monies and possessions on her. During the marriage, Cornwall was never far from her thoughts. She made further donations to her native village, including wagon loads of clothing for the poor, and dresses for her mother.

After John Gall's death, more suitors appeared on the scene, and in 1479 Thomasine became Mrs John Percival. The following year John Percival was made a Sherriff of the City of London, and to record this great event, Thomasine is reputed to have had a 'road' built from Lanstephadon — Launceston — to the Atlantic coast, by way of Green-a-moor, Week Ford, and through Poundstock to either Wansum or Melhuc Mouth. It was, of course, not the kind of road we know today, but a hard surface of stones filled with earth. It did, however, make an easier journey for the men, horses and carts that carried sand and seaweed from the beach to their farms inland: a practice which continued for centuries.

Thomasine donated a further forty marks towards the building of a tower to Stephen's Church at Launceston, asking that the pinnacles be high enough to be seen from Swannacott Farm, some twelve miles away. Did perhaps the memory of her cousin John Dineham linger uncomfortably in her conscience?

In 1498, John Percival was made Lord Mayor of London and knighted by the King. So our Cornish shepherd girl became Lady Thomasine.

Her marriage to Sir John lasted a quarter of a century. He died in 1504, and for her last thirty years Thomasine remained a widow. During her generous lifetime she was responsible for building a number of bridges and repairing roads in North Cornwall.

In death she was generous too. When she departed this life at the great age of 89, she made her cousin John Dineham, the Monk of St Cleer, legatee, and left £20 to her brother, John Bonaventure, as well as two shillings and two pence to the Clergy of Stratton Church for bread and wine to be consumed on 'Remembrance Day', when prayers were to be said for her soul.

Not all her money came down to Cornwall: there were legacies in London for the supply of candles, the repair of church ornaments, and for food and drink on the anniversaries of her death and those of her husbands.

It is an interesting coincidence that the four men who featured in her life, her three husbands and the young man who turned his back on the outside world when sne did not come back home, were all called John.

Thomasine built a College at Week St Mary: '. . . parts of the building remain . . . a section of battlemented wall . . .'

One of her biggest gifts was the creation of a Trust, from which a School or College was built at Week St Mary for the purpose of educating the sons of Gentlemen of Cornwall and Devon. The Headmaster, Mr Cholwill, was to receive a stipend of £12 a year, and a laundress was to be paid 13/4 (about 66p in modern currency) for washing the clothes of the Headmaster and other teachers.

Parts of the building remain: principally a recessed doorway, a section of the battlemented wall, a well and the steps leading to the platform from which the school bell rung. Intriguingly, over the doorway of a nearby cottage there is a large letter 'T'. The practical people of this world will say it is a clue relating to the name of the builder.

But some of us like to think it relates to Thomasine. Far fetched? But then this whole factual story could be described as just that.

Either way, as long as there is Week St Mary, the shepherd girl who went to London will be remembered.

The church and its stately tower were probably built by Thomasine, or at least she would have contributed largely towards their building.

This, the northern corner of Cornwall, is inhabited by a number of ghosts. If she haunts this parish then it is surely a kindly spirit and, who knows, all these years on, the spirits of Thomasine and Cousin John may now be joined.

Eccentric Architecture

'Here one is reaching not only the end of Cornwall, but, it seems, the end of the world.'

That was Sir John Betjeman's impression of Morwenstow.

I know what he means: Morwenstow has an *other* worldly quality. For me there is a refreshing, renewing power about the place. This is Hawker country, and something of the man's spirit seems to linger on.

Parson and poet, author and creator of the Harvest Festival service, Robert Stephen Hawker was a character of many parts. His exploits coping with shipwrecked sailors made him a legend in his lifetime; while his earthly end, as a death-bed Roman Catholic convert, is still filled with controversy and confusion. It is incredible to think Hawker's bones are not resting in this churchyard he loved so dearly. For more than four decades he presided here.

He came, in the words of a contributor to *John Bull*, 'to a manse in ruins and partly used as a barn; a parish peopled by wreckers and dissenting Bryanites; and a venerable church, deserted and ill-cared for amidst a heap of weeds and nettles.'

At considerable personal expense he built and maintained a school in the parish — how sad he would be to find it now closed — he was responsible for building King William's Bridge and the parish church he transformed. In the field of church finance, it was Hawker who first understood the importance of the weekly offertory.

Materially, though, his most impressive legacy is the vicarage, which is now a private house and almost part of the churchyard, rather Gothic, rising like something from an Iris Murdoch novel, and set among trees. The chimneys are remarkable in that they represent the towers of churches with which he was associated and Oxford colleges; an exception is the kitchen chimney, representing his mother's tomb. Above the front door of the vicarage are these words: 'A house, a glebe, a pound a day; a pleasant place to watch and pray. Be true to Church, be kind to poor, O Minister for evermore.'

The vicarage and grounds possess a remarkable serenity considering that the Atlantic and a frequently storm-battered coastline are only four furlongs away. Roughly halfway between Bude and Hartland, there is no village at this point: simply the church, the vicarage, the Bush Inn, and an aged farm, now partly tearoom and partly shop, which also provides accommodation for visitors.

I make regular visits to Morwenstow on business, and if the time permits I try to spend a few minutes in the church, and always I take a distant look at the vicarage through the trees. It is a lovely monument to a great Westcountry cleric and eccentric.

Cornwall does in fact boast some beautifully eccentric architecture.

Morwenstow Vicarage: '. . . the chimneys represent towers of churches with which Hawker was associated . . .'

Falmouth has one of my special favourites: Jacob's Ladder. A vast granite stairway, with one hundred and eleven steps — I can assure you of the number because I have counted them — it climbs from The Moor to Vernon Place. Why Jacob's Ladder? Visitors must ask themselves that question. It all goes back to one Jacob Hamblyn who conceived the idea of this bizarre creation. He was an important figure in the town in 1791 when the Wesleyan church was built. Near the top of those steep steps was a group of cottages known appropriately as Mount Zion cottages — though it is possible they took their name from the nearby Jewish synagogue.

Tradition has it that Sir Walter Raleigh smoked his first tobacco in public in Falmouth, as a guest of the famous Killigrew family at Arwenack Manor. But I suspect the ghost of Sir Walter later haunted the Killigrews because they did two despicable things — despicable that is to a tobacco man. They built Falmouth's first Custom House which was to extract revenue from imported tobacco — and, worse still, a King's Pipe was constructed to burn illegally imported tobacco, chewing and smoking varieties, cigars and cigarettes. But knowing the Cornish love of evasion, one can only guess that a lot did not go up in smoke. Anyway, the King's Pipe remains in Falmouth today: an intriguing piece of architecture, an historic legacy of those illicit imports.

Chapel Street in Penzance is one of the great streets of Cornwall. When you walk down Chapel Street, you're walking amidst genuine Cornish history. Marie Brontë, mother of the literary Brontë sisters, was born here. The Turk's Head, dating back to the thirteenth century, is the oldest inn in Penzance. The Union Hotel is famous because from the Minstrel Gallery in its dining room, the death of Lord Nelson and the Victory of Trafalgar were announced. History indeed stalks this street. St Mary's Church and the Wesleyan chapel, the Nautical Museum and The Georgian House, once the home of Mayors of Penzance, are only some of the fascinating features of Chapel Street.

But its special curiosity is Egyptian House. Built around 1835 to accommodate a geological collection, after years of neglect it was sensitively restored by the Landmark Trust in 1973 and is now a

Jacob's Ladder, Falmouth: 'A vast granite stairway, with one hundred and eleven steps . . .' ▶

National Trust property. In a sentence, it's just about the most unusual shop in the whole of the South West.

I stood in front of it recently and was reminded of Foulston's Egyptian Forester's Hall in Devonport, just across the Tamar. I am no architect, but surely the same spirit created these two strange buildings. In terms of sheer style, they seem close relations. This creation in Chapel Street is a replica of the Egyptian Hall in London.

Edgar Rees, in his *Old Penzance* which appeared in 1956, wrote: 'It was, I believe, erected for Mr George Lavin to house his large collection of minerals. During her visit to Penzance many years ago, Lady Burdett Coutts purchased the whole collection, and it is said that from the money received for the minerals, Mr Lavin built the hotel adjoining the Queen's Hotel on the sea front. It was called "Lavin's Hotel" up to the time of it being sold to Mr Charles Ball, who renamed it "Mount's Bay Hotel".'

Another Penzance curiosity is The Abbey Hotel, just off Chapel Street, standing in sloping Abbey Street. It is one of the oldest and most delightful buildings in the town. Largely seventeenth century in character, it is currently owned by the former model, Jean Shrimpton, one of the most famous and photographed figures of the swinging sixties. But the Abbey is something of a mystery in that its previous owner, an architect, author and journalist, failed to fathom its earliest history. There is a strong local tradition, however, that it was linked, in some monastic way, to St Michael's Mount. It got a mention in Gilbert's *History of Cornwall*: 'There is in Penzance an ancient building called The Abbey which is supposed to be dedicated to religion. It is now the property of the Borlase family . . .' In 1825 this grand old building was restored and was improved with the adding of a drawing room on the garden side and the installation of the sash windows with 'Gothic' glazing bars — happily these features remain, adding character and age to the present day Abbey.

The Poet Laureate, on a visit to Penzance in the sixties, commented on the good quality of modern development hereabouts by private individuals — and this corner of the town is an excellent

Egyptian House, Penzance: '. . . just about the most unusual shop in the whole of the South West.' ▶

STUDIO TWO
5

The First and Last House at Land's End and (right) The Abbey House, Penzance, currently owned by former model, Jean Shrimpton.

example and an object lesson for many Corporations.

There has to be a first and last — in most things anyway — and one of my favourite bits of Penwith architecture happens to be both: the first and last house at Land's End, not to be confused with the First & Last Inn, standing alongside Sennen Church in Sennen village.

Land's End: the very words fire the imagination. Written or spoken, they have a magical magnetic quality.

Joe Poynton, the Penzance architect, tells me there was a shepherd's hut originally on the site of the first and last house which stands alone on the cliffs. 'The building goes back to the 1600s,' he explained. 'There are definite seventeenth-century characteristics, and it was used by one Matthew Thomas of Boswednack near Zennor who kept sheep at Land's End . . . he used it until the property became part of the Estate.'

The earliest photograph of the house, taken some time in the 1860s shows it as a refreshment house run by Grace Thomas of Sennen who, during the summer months, walked out here carrying

White's St Columb Rectory with its moat — 'one of the most picturesque in the whole dioscese.'

her produce and refreshments. Clearly the seeds of Cornish tourism had already been sown.

William White, the architect who was born in 1825 and died in 1900, may not have been an eccentric but he has left a distinctive legacy in Cornwall, and no traveller among interesting Cornish architecture can ignore him or his work — working as he did on something like twenty major sites. Some of his most distinctive marks remain in and around St Columb.Thanks to William White, St Columb has a special niche in Westcountry architecture.

His first St Columb client was one Dr Samuel Edmund Walker who wanted the old Rectory rebuilt, not only for himself, the incumbent, but as a possible Bishop's Palace. Around the middle of the last century, politics in the Cornish Church were largely angled on the location of the Cathedral; with Bodmin and Truro rivalling for that accolade, St Columb was suggested as a third alternative—but it was not to be. Nevertheless White's St Columb Rectory with

Trewan Hall, St Columb, a sixteenth-century manor restored by William White.

William White's Bank built in 1857 in St Columb — now a solicitor's office.

its moat is undoubtedly one of the most picturesque in the whole diocese. Today it performs a different role: the Old Rectory Hotel and Country Club, standing in two acres of peaceful well laid-out gardens, still manages to generate the style and elegance of other more leisurely days.

William White, who was born in Northampton but began his career in Truro, was something of a revolutionary in his Victorian heyday: an architect capable of producing modern progressive designs. His bank, built in 1857, is another notable St Columb landmark; later used by the Ministry of Labour it is now a solicitor's office. With brown and multicoloured stones and coloured bands of red brick, it's rated one of the finest Victorian Gothic buildings west of the Tamar.

Other White legacies in the area are Penmellyn, a delightful slate house on the northern shoulder of the town, and Trewan Hall, a splendid sixteenth-century manor which he restored.

All four remain today: living reminders of William White's vision and vitality: no ordinary creator, a man who once said 'Style as such must be thrown to the winds . . .'—and who meant it.

Port Isaac somehow manages to retain an old-world charm. The nooks and the crannies intensify the impression; nothing more so than 'Squeezibelly Alley' which, in places, is little more than eighteen inches wide. It leads from the main sloping street through the middle of someone's house, and more formally is known as Temple Bar.

Times were when Port Isaac was a busy fishing port with its own boat-building yards. The quay here was built in the reign of Henry VII, and the view up the coast to Tintagel Headland I rate one of the finest in Cornwall.

When we first came to North Cornwall in the mid 1960s, our fishman, who called on us at Bossiney, was Jerry Sweet, a great Port Isaac character, who was quite convinced decimalization 'wouldn't catch on', and insisted on charging us in the old currency of pounds, shillings and pence! Jerry had an interesting theory

The Bird Cage, an oddly-shaped house in Port Isaac, left, in an Edwardian post card; right, in 1982.

about the huddled nature of the Port Isaac buildings—something he enjoyed because he didn't have a lot of time for officialdom, whether it came in the form of planning permission or modern currency. Jerry's fascinating theory was that the closeness of the cottages enabled the families to tap warnings to one another about the arrival of press gangs. He also reasoned that the cramped shape of Port Isaac made it an ideal spot for smugglers in that a smuggler could nip into the front door of a cottage and out of the back and be in another street in a matter of seconds. Port Isaac, with its architectural jig-saw puzzle, must have been a headache for the preventive men.

Another peculiar piece of Port Isaac architecture is The Bird Cage, an oddly shaped house acquired by the National Trust and now let as holiday accommodation. The two illustrations here show the building as depicted on an Edwardian postcard and photographed in October 1982.

But the most dramatic building—one of the most beautiful too—hereabouts on this North Cornish coast is the Regent Gothic folly on Doyden Point at Port Quin. It was, in fact, used as the residence of Dr Dwight Enys in the first Poldark series on BBC television.

Left: Squeezibelly Alley at Port Isaac
Below: The Folly at Doyden, Port Quin.

Curiosities in the Landscape

Nature is a great sculptor. The fact is there are some fantastic shapes along and around the Penwith coastline, and one of the most beautiful is the Irish Lady, 'a peculiar and pleasing rock' at Land's End. According to an ancient legend, an Irish ship was once wrecked there and all lives were lost, save for an Irish Lady who clung to the rock. Local fishermen—always a superstitious breed—in times past claimed they saw her ghost. Moreover the Irish Lady really lives up to her name in that her graceful rocky outline does suggest a lady in a long black cloak going down into the sea.

Land's End, of course, carries many echoes from the past. According to one eerie tale, the figure of a man once stood on the point and a prophetic tradition insisted that it would fall at a time of disaster—and it did just that on 30 January 1649, the day King Charles was beheaded. Furthermore on the very same day a ship, carrying the King's treasure and furniture, broke from its moorings and was wrecked at Godrevy in St Ives Bay.

Another strange prophecy is linked to Table-Men, which means Rock Table, nearby in the parish of Sennen. This large flat stone is said to have been where the seven Saxon Kings dined together, and Merlin the wizard, who advised Arthur, added to speculation by predicting that even more Kings will gather around Table-Men before some impressive event—or the end of the world.

Some people may argue that our Cornish crosses—the most familiar of our antiquities—are too well-known, too obvious to be called 'curiosities'. That may be so, but one cross in particular is a curious character. The cross at the road juntion near Boskenna, is mounted on a stone roller *and* a cider press.

'Land's End carries many echoes from the past.' ▶

Cornwall, and Penwith in particular, are inhabited by some strange shapes, and I resolved to visit a few of them.

It was autumn—a good time to explore the Cornish countryside—the coastline too for that matter, and I continued my journey among the strange stones at Catchall, a first meeting with The Blind Fiddler. The old story goes that the blind fiddler was turned into this stone for playing his fiddle on a Sunday. This is a thread running through a number of our stones and folklore. Why? The question is inevitable, but the answer is by no means 100 per cent cast-iron. Some say that when Christians and Pagans were battling with one another, the Christians put about such stories to influence people, and to encourage them to turn away from 'the old religion'. Others say the explanation is more recent, dating from the Puritans who turned up their high moral noses on the subject of singing and dancing. Either way, The Blind Fiddler remains an impressive albeit puzzling stone, just under eleven feet in height.

From Catchall I moved on to Chun Quoit. It loomed up like some big mysterious mushroom. In a way, these stones are infuriating characters, witnesses to a distant past, yet retaining their secrets.

Below: Table-Men where Saxon Kings dined. Right: Cross near Boskenna mounted on a stone roller and a cider press.

Chun Quoit (above) looked like a big mysterious mushroom. The Blind Fiddler (right) with horses ploughing in the background — a rare sight.

Maybe I should have brought a psychic with me to Chun—for I am sure this noble quoit would have a fascinating tale to tell.

I have been interested in psychometry for a number of years, since meeting a lady by the name of Betty Lukey who gave me a remarkable 'reading' through psychometry—in that instance through holding my wrist watch in her hands and picking up vibrations, feelings and images from that object which I had worn for several years. The cynic will naturally scoff, but aided only by her gift and that wrist watch she revealed some things from my past with amazing accuracy, and, even more incredibly, predicted things relating to my private and working lives that have come true.

This astonishing arrangement of slabs of stone that make Chun Quoit—sometimes called Cromlech and sometimes Dolmen—are believed to be the remains of burial chambers from long ago. There is evidence too that they were once covered by mounds of earth.

From Chun I moved on to Zennor Quoit, high above Zennor village, invisible from the road, but less than a mile away as the Cornish Chough supposedly flew. Even in its ruined condition—due to the vandalism of a farmer I'm told—Zennor Quoit still manages to generate a certain majesty. Someone has said that in Penwith

you can find yourself walking among 'the early instalments of history'. I felt just that as I came face to face with this great battered dolmen. Zennor Quoit can only be roughly dated, somewhere between 2000 and 1500 years before the stable birth at Bethlehem. Bodies of the dead were laid here. Originally the Quoit had seven side slabs and terminals, but the huge capstone has been wrenched from its supports and is now propped against them. There is a theory that a local farmer wanted to use the stones for cattle shelters and one can only guess he erected those four stone posts nearby.

To move from the Hundred of Penwith to Bodmin Moor is to travel from one Cornish Kingdom to another.

Bodmin Moor is full of mystery containing some fascinating curiosities. On the fringe of it stands King Doniert's Stone, in the parish of St Cleer, just off the Redgate-Minions road. This is one of the most impressive of our inscribed stones. An ornamented cross-base, the inscription reads *Doniert rogavit pro anima*, which

Zennor Quoit (below) even in its ruined condition still manages to generate a certain majesty. Right: King Doniert's Stone in the parish of St Cleer.

KING DONIERTS
STONE
ANCIENT MONUMENT

translated means 'Doniert has asked—prayers—for his soul'. Alongside it stands a cross shaft, decorated with interlacing work.

Doniert was drowned in the River Fowey in the valley below, in the year 878. A lovely innocent-looking ribbon of water most days; when I travel along the valley I sometimes wonder how such a seemingly harmless character as the river could have done such a thing as kill a King. When you handle King Doniert's Stone, it can be a moving moment, because you are in touch with the Dark Ages. A visit here somehow makes those Dark Ages less dark, less distant.

Some say Doniert was the last Cornish King, but Charles Woolf in his excellent *The Archaeology of Cornwall* suggests this may not be the case:

'Doniert is reputed to have been the last of the Cornish kings for the Saxons had already defeated the Cornish in the east by AD 838. In the extreme west, however, there is evidence that there was at least one who ruled at a later date. There is a cross outside Penlee House in Penzance, which at one time stood in the market-place. Although it has a more ancient appearance, it is dated to the tenth century AD. On its reverse, at the bottom left-hand corner, is the inscription *Regis Ricati Crux* —the cross of King Ricatus. Beyond the validity of the name, nothing is known of Ricatus but in spite of the Saxon success in the east of the county, he could well have ruled after Dumgarth since he was in the far west which the Saxons had not yet reached.'

Now my journey took me out to the North Cornish coast—to Arthur's legendary land at Tintagel or, more precisely, Bossiney, because in history and in character Bossiney is not Tintagel.

The old rotten borough of Bossiney, which once sent Sir Francis Drake to Parliament, possesses a genuine natural curiosity. The Petrifying Well stands in a sloping field above Bossiney Cove; it is a tiny spring of water which issues from a mossy rock and has the strange quality of turning vegetation, slowly but surely, into stone!

Down in the cove itself is another Bossiney 'character': Elephant Rock, looking for all the world like an elephant facing the Atlantic or, in the eye of imagination, standing at the door of some Hindu temple.

◄**Elephant Rock, Bossiney**

This North Cornish coast is peopled with some really fascinating shapes. Profile Rock at Boscastle Harbour, for example, from certain angles uncannily resembles the severe features of Queen Victoria. Moreover if you are at Boscastle Harbour an hour before low tide, you can see and *hear* the blow hole which sends a spectacular cloud of spray cascading with a remarkably loud report across the harbour. One visiting writer, in an imaginative moment, christened it 'The Devil's Elbows'.

Another curious rock formation on the cliff path which links Boscastle and Tintagel is the Lady's Window, 'a perforated rocky crag, sharply silhouetted against the sky'. If you have a head for heights, you may be tempted to step through the narrow—very narrow—ledge and look down some two hundred metres to the sea. Also nearby is a strange 'terrace' of heather-peppered cliffs. By my reckoning, this is one of the finest stretches of coastal scenery in all Cornwall.

The coastline below Tintagel too wears some weird and wonderful

The Petrifying Well at Bossiney (below) 'has the strange quality of turning vegetation into stone.' 'Profile Rock (right) at Boscastle . . . uncannily resembles the features of Queen Victoria.'

faces. 'It is', wrote W.J.C. Armstrong, 'as if giants had been tearing at a rocky face and flinging debris anywhere and everywhere, here cutting the face clean, as if with a guillotine, there leaving a pinnacle like Cleopatra's Needle . . .'

That lonely pinnacle on the cliffs by Trebarwith was, in fact, left there for good reasons. My old friend Allen Menhenick, who worked on the quarry out here on the cliffs, told me: 'When "crib" time came the quarry men needed some shelter in bad weather and sheltered behind it.' Crib is an old Cornish expression, meaning a break with something to eat and drink.

Finally, on this excursion, I came back inland again on the suggestion of a reader who told me that one line of stones close to St Columb always generated—for her at least—a haunted quality.

Devon possesses a class of monument which we do not have in our Cornish landscape: parallel lines of stones. The nearest thing are The Nine Maidens near St Columb; the stones here though are in one line only. They point in the direction of a monolith called The Old Man or Voel Maen—the goal stone—and there is an ancient tradition that the others are running a race towards it. Were they too punished for indulging in some sport on a Sunday? William Borlase came across them in the 1700s and referred to them as 'The Nine Maids'. Anyway, they remain today; a unique Cornish colony, standing in a still straight line.

Anne Jeffries of St Teath: Witch or Saint?

Sonia and I live in a cottage called Land's End. On the other side of the green valley is the village of St Teath—in pronunciation Teath rhymes with death. A hill village, high above the Allen Valley, this is a haunted corner of North Cornwall. When the wind is in a certain quarter, they say you can hear the cries of Squire Cheney's ghost hounds out hunting.

Inevitably then I find myself including Anne Jeffries in Cornish curiosities. In a way, she selects herself because she was indeed a curious character. Yet for the first nineteen years, Anne Jeffries lived a seemingly average life for a girl of her background. Born at St Teath in December 1626, the daughter of a local labourer, she became a servant to the Moses Pitt family, who lived in a large house in the village.

Then, one day, she had what some people at first may have thought was a fit or a dream or a nightmare—or all three. Anne was convinced she had been transported to some magical place where she met fairies, miniature folk in green. For one whole winter the poor girl remained in a delirious state. Today she would have been sent to a psychiatrist, possibly ending up in a mental hospital. But her people let Nature take its course. She seemed to have been transformed into some witless character—a mere shadow of the girl they once knew; incredibly, though, by the following summer she had recovered. There was, however, an important difference: Anne now believed her 'visitations' to be a kind of magic. But it was an accident that produced the biggest revelation. Moses Pitt's mother fell in the garden, badly injuring herself and Anne, discovering she possessed healing hands, cured her immediately.

She claimed she was not only conversing with the little folk, but they were instructing her in herbal matters. In fact she could neither read nor write; nevertheless news of her healing powers spread like a forest fire, and sick people from London to Land's End made their way to St Teath to see her.

Of Anne's cures, Sabine Baring-Gould later reflected: '. . . they are to be put in the same category of faith cures all the world over, whether performed at Lourdes, or by the Christian Scientists, or by Shamans in the Steppes of Tartary.'

Anne was reputed to tell the future too. St Teath gossip even said she could make herself invisible! Anne, however, was unlucky in that she lived in an age obsessed with witch-hunting—and at a period in British history when the nation was bitterly divided in Civil War. Unfortunately she was indiscreet enough to go about St Teath in the midst of the struggle praying very much and bidding 'people keepe ye old form of prayer; she says the King shall shortly enjoye his own, and be revenged on his enemyes'. Such words were bound to offend those who sided with Cromwell. Predictably she made enemies among the Cornish establishment, a notable one in the person of John Tregeagle JP, a strong Cromwell supporter, and a steward to Lord Robartes of Lanhydrock House, who obtained a warrant and succeeded in getting Anne committed to Bodmin Gaol, an infamous cage for criminals. Despite being deprived of food for part of her sentence, Anne not only avoided the dreaded gaol fever but even appeared to thrive. It was rumoured she was being fed by 'small people cladd in greene and sometimes by birds'.

The evidence against the young woman must have been flimsy because she was released from Bodmin, and soon after married a Padstow man. There, on the other side of the Camel Estuary, they settled down and she continued her healing work, never charging a penny for her services.

A witch or a Saint?

Looking at her roughly 350 years on, Anne Jeffries may have been something of both.

Some Strange Sporting Facts

It is an odd fact that whereas Cornish Rugby has produced as many as 28 England internationals—admittedly not all of them natives—only one Cornishman has played test cricket for England, and equally, a solitary native has worn the England shirt in international soccer.

The rugger record is a remarkable one, even allowing for the fact that Rugby in Cornwall—for many—is almost a religion or way of life. Yet there is an enigmatic quality about the Rugby pattern too. For all the passion and the galaxy of individual talent, our Cornwall team has only won the county championship on one occasion, and that was as long ago as 1908.

Our one test cricketer was Jack Frederick Crapp who was born at St Columb in 1912. He grew into a sound phlegmatic left-hand batsman for Gloucestershire and an outstanding slip fielder. Moreover, when he left the playing field, he became a highly respected umpire in the first-class game. His test appearances for England were restricted to a mere seven matches, and he had the misfortune to encounter Australian pace and fury at their height in the persons of Ray Lindwall and Keith Miller, one of the great fast bowling combinations in the history of the game. Nevertheless in those seven test matches he managed to average 29 runs.

Jack Crapp's achievements for Gloucestershire in county cricket were substantial—by any standards. In a career that stretched from the summer of 1936 to 1956—Hitler robbed him of some of his golden years—he amassed an aggregate of more than 23,000 runs, averaging 35.03, and making in the process as many as 39 centuries.

Our only soccer international was Raymond Bowden of Looe who first hit the sporting headlines as a promising right-winger for Liskeard Grammar School. But his goal-scoring power and appetite were such that he switched to centre-forward. He was quickly

Left: Jack Crapp
Above: Raymond Bowden
Below: Polhilsa Farm, boxer Len Harvey's birth place, near Stoke Climsland.

spotted by Bob Jack, the manager of Plymouth Argyle. At Home Park, Raymond Bowden was a tremendous success, scoring 83 goals in 146 league matches.

He made a great impression in the Plymouth and District League when only fourteen years of age. In his fifteenth year in League and Cup games he netted in the region of 100 goals, scoring ten in one game against Tavistock. In the same season he was the principal reason for Looe reaching the final of the Cornwall Senior Cup. Yet members of the Looe Committee hesitated about playing him in the Final, thinking an older player of greater physique might be better equipped for the hurly-burly of the Cup Final. It is said young Bowden was chosen by a majority of just one vote — and on the day he scored both his team's goals to win the Cup by two goals to one against Newquay.

Perhaps inevitably Argyle were unable to retain his services, and he was transferred to Arsenal, one of the great clubs of the 1930s, 'lucky Arsenal' as they were unfairly called by those envious of their reputation and success. It was while wearing the Arsenal colours that Raymond Bowden became an England player. Bowden moved to Newcastle United in 1938 whom he captained, but, like Jack Crapp, he lost vital seasons to the war, an event which shortened his career.

I once asked Percy Bartlett, then Secretary of the CCFA, and 'Mr Football' in Cornwall, how he rated Raymond Bowden. 'Undoubtedly the finest footballer Cornwall has produced,' was his reply.

Fred Peel-Yates is known under three names. For more than thirty years he has made a huge contribution to Westcountry sports journalism. Since 1950 he has written a weekly sports column for *The Cornish Guardian* under the pen name of Fan-Fare, and as Westheath he has written for *The Western Evening Herald* since 1949. The son of a Cornish parson, who played Rugby for Cornwall, Fred has probably produced more words on Cornish sport than any man alive. He lives at Bodmin, was involved in soccer administration for a number of years, and still enjoys a round of golf at St Enodoc.

I asked him about Cornwall's lack of success in the higher echelons of sport.

'Some years back I wrote that sports-wise an iron curtain comes down at Plymouth and any activity west of the Tamar was mainly confined to making pasties or putting up "Bed and Breakfast" signs! Indeed, a real knowledge of Cornwall is still so limited that one TV announcer blithely informed us that Truro was the county town,' he replied. 'Cocooned in such ignorance the urge to break into the sporting Big Time has over the years produced few outstanding names to conjure with. So far as Association Football is concerned, the Football League scouts seem to be thin on the top in Cornwall. It's doubtful if any of them ever watch youth or schoolboy football in these parts, and *that* is the breeding ground for potential top-class talent. Coaching facilities, too, are strictly limited and that goes for cricket as well. Bodmin's Geoff Cocks was offered trials with Bristol Rovers when he was in his mid-twenties, but turned it down. Another Bodmin man, John Shirley, did have trials with Rovers, but he too was then in his middle twenties, too late to start a career in professional soccer. Back to cricket: and perhaps the present set-up of the Cornwall Cricket League may be partly to blame for the lack of potential top grade players down here. Surely an inclusive Senior 1 set-up to include the best from the east and the west might in the end produce highter standards all round.

We may have been an insular county in pre-war days, but we no longer deserve to have that tag. But until the rest of England decides to take a real hard look at us we will still have only one foot on the first rung of the sporting ladder.'

Perhaps the most extraordinary sporting fact relating to Cornwall is that a Cornishman is the only British boxer to have held the most coveted title in the fight game: Heavyweight Champion of the World.

Bob Fitzsimmons first saw the light of day in a thatched cottage in Wendron Street, Helston. He left Cornwall at the age of two and was brought up in New Zealand, but here in Cornwall we naturally count him as one of us. A Cornishman of iron constitution, his name will live for ever in Boxing's Hall of Fame — and lives on in Helston in the shape of the Fitzsimmons Arms in Coinagehall Street. He is remembered too with a plaque outside his cottage birthplace.

In a fighting career which covered three decades, Fitzsimmons became the first boxer to hold three world titles. At the age of 35, he became Heavyweight Champion, knocking out Gentleman Jim Corbett with his famous solar plexus punch. Then he took the Middleweight crown by knocking out the great Jack Dempsey, and, later still, at the age of 41, he battled bravely through twenty rounds to become the Light Heavyweight Champion, thus completing an extraordinary hat-trick. He went on fighting professionally to the age of 51, and died three years later of pneumonia at the age of 54, in Chicago. He was an outstanding defensive fighter, a reputation underlined by the fact that he died with an unscarred face.

A less well-known fact is that another son of Cornwall won great distinction in the boxing ring. Len Harvey, rated by some experts as the greatest British boxer in this century, was born at Polhilsa Farm Cottage, near Stoke Climsland, on 11 July 1907.

In a career which spanned the years 1920 to 1942, the Cornishman fought twenty title fights and won a Lord Lonsdale Belt outright. Three times Len Harvey was in the ring fighting for a world title crown, and in 1939 he was recognised by the British Boxing Board of Control as the Light Heavyweight Champion of the World.

Harvey began boxing professionally before his thirteenth birthday, when he was paid five shillings for six rounds. His brilliant boxing — like Bob Fitzsimmons he had a superlative defence — earned him the title 'Britain's Wonder Boxer' when still in his teens. In over three hundred fights he was only beaten eleven times — three of which were hotly disputed verdicts — while his final defeat was when he had been out of the ring for three years and was a Pilot Officer in the Royal Air Force. This, at the hands of Freddie Mills, was sadly and ironically the only time he was knocked out in 418 contests.

An outstanding ambassador for boxing, Len Harvey was a gentleman and sportsman. He fought cleanly and was never disqualified. In and out of the ring he worked hard to make boxing an honourable career.

In their very differing styles, Bob Fitzsimmons and Len Harvey then represent two very substantial contributions from Cornwall to the world of sport. In the case of Fitzsimmons it remains a unique achievement, and in the case of Harvey, the contribution was deeper and more significant than the sheer brilliance of his boxing skills.

But Cornwall's most distinctive feature on the sporting scene is arguably Cornish wrestling — 'wrastling' as the true Cornish call it. The sport, which has a long history, is very different from that brand regularly paraded on our television screens.

Nobody is absolutely sure about the genesis of Cornish wrestling, but historians tell us that at the Battle of Agincourt, where banners depicted the different county contingents, the Cornishmen had two wrestlers on theirs. Richard Trevithick, who invented a high-pressure steam engine by the age of 25, was an excellent wrestler, and it is good to report that the sport is alive and well today.

The Cornu-Breton matches, in particular, have a real Celtic flavour. The ritual before these championships can be impressive with the Wrestlers' Oath being spoken in four languages: English and Cornish, French and Breton.

'In the boom days of mining, most of our wrestlers tended to come from the mining territory of West Cornwall, but as the mines declined and china clay grew in importance, the wrestlers emerged from the china clay country. Now however the recruitment is spread over the county.' So Bryan Kendall told me when we talked at Perranporth. Bryan, who has served the sport well both as wrestler and administrator for more than twenty years, said: 'Cornish wrestling is in very good health, but not, of course, as strong as it was in say the 1920s. Today you're competing against many other sports and pastimes, things like golf and sailing that in the old days were pretty exclusive.

'In Cornwall today we've about 50 or 60 wrestlers; whereas in Brittany the number runs into thousands. All the same we usually give them a very good run for their money!

Delabole — A Deep Hole

Delabole is famous on the strength of its slate and quarry. Indeed they gave birth and name to the North Cornish village — and vital employment to generations of Cornishmen in the area.

Reputed to be the oldest and largest slate quarry in England, it has been worked for more than four hundred years and, according to *The Guinness Book of Records,* is the deepest man-made hole in Europe, more than 500 feet deep and over a mile in circumference. Delabole Quarry is, in fact, the only example of large-scale slate quarrying outside North Wales and the Lake District.

Delabole slate is a versatile durable material with excellent weathering characteristics. In the form of roof slates, tombstones, gateposts and boundary walls, it has helped to shape the face of North Cornwall. The slate is quarried by blasting and cut to width by diamond-tipped saws.

In the reign of the first Elizabeth, the quarries were of prime importance, and Carew, writing in 1602 in his *Survey of Cornwall,* referred to Delabole slate as 'in substance thin, in colour fair, weight light, in lasting long and generally carrieth good regard . . . great store is yearly conveyed by shipping both to other parts of the realm and also beyond the seas to Britanny and the Netherlands'.

Before the coming of the railways in the 1890s, the slate was hauled six twisting miles to Port Gaverne. As many as thirty wagons and one hundred horses were employed to load a sixty ton vessel lying on the beach at Port Gaverne. In those days the sea was the highway for Westcountry commerce. The brittle slates were passed from hand to hand, a careful painstaking operation, down to

◀ Cornish wrestling at St Minver 1982. The man on the right is the 'stickler', a kind of referee.

An earlier view of Delabole Quarry: Above left: a few men can lever massive slabs of slate. Below left: the inclined railway. Above: paving slabs. Below: loading the carts for transport to the coast. Back cover: loading the slates on board ship at Port Gaverne.

the vessels where the slates were then packed between layers of hay in the hold.

In 1914 Delabole achieved literary fame when Eden Philpotts wrote his novel *Old Delabole* which he dedicated to Thomas Hardy. Now a rare book, it contains some marvellously descriptive passages on the life and landscape of those days.

The late Ronald Duncan, the poet, playwright and farmer from near Morwenstow, on occasions said some harsh things about Cornwall and the Cornish. But he always wrote beautifully, always with a poet's feeling for words and aware of the magic they can weave. He, perhaps more than any other writer, got to the heart of Delabole slate in three simple sentences: 'There is no inscription on a slab of Delabole. It bears no silly rhyme or motto, or any mark of this or any age. It is what it is, and in its primeval remoteness it makes a comment on what we are.'

I recommend a visit to the Quarry for the reason that it's a bit of real working Cornwall: a chance to see Cornish industry at close range. Slate splitting and dressing are demonstrated in the museum, and there are some grand old tools on display; equipment, photographs and quarry products are all there.

Looking down into this deep pit is a strange experience, like being part of some lunar landscape, and there on the edge of the Quarry, you wonder just how many million years have passed since this slate was formed in some strange fold of the earth's crust. You come away with the realisation that time itself is a very curious thing.

Customs: Cornish and Curious

Every Cornish calendar is unique.

Traditional events and customs, though, have given each year a shape and a pattern. In this section we look at some of our curious customs, a number of which have sadly disappeared, and we Cornish are poorer for their loss. Ours is a rich heritage, and when something distinctly Cornish goes it is as if a part of our Celtic identity has been chipped away.

Here are some details relating to Hall Monday — Nicky-nan Night — contained in the *Reports of the Royal Institution of Cornwall,* published in 1842:

'On the day termed "Hall" Monday, which precedes Shrove Tuesday, about the dusk of the evening it is the custom for boys, and, in some cases, for those above the age of boys, to prowl about the streets with short clubs, and to knock loudly at every door, running off to escape detection on the slightest sign of a motion within. If, however, no attention be excited, and especially if any article be discovered negligently exposed, or carelessly guarded, then the things are carried away; and on the following morning are seen displayed in some conspicuous place, to expose the disgraceful want of vigilance supposed to characterise the owner. The time when this is practised is called "Nicky-nan-night"; and the individuals concerned are supposed to represent some imps of darkness, that seize on, and expose unguarded moments.'

Midsummer Day has always been a highlight in the Cornish calendar, and Jonathan Couch dealt with it in his fascinating *History of Polperro,* published in 1871. 'What Hallowe'en is to the Scotch, this day is to us; the season of love divination. The youth of both sexes, but especially, say some, the girls meet; those who have sweethearts to determine whether they are constant, and those whose choice is yet unfixed, to enquire whom they are fated to marry. There are many methods of consulting the future practised on this day. Some of the oracles are consulted plainly; others require many preparatory ceremonies. Sometimes the actual presence of the wished-for lover is manifested, at other times the answer is vouchsafed by dreams. I subjoin a few of the forms of divination for the use of those who may need them.

'On Midsummer morning get up early and go into the woods and fields in search of one of those rarities, an even-leaved ash, or clover. If so lucky as to find it, carry it about you; as an old couplet assures you that with:

Even-leaved ash or four-leaved clover,
You'll meet your true love before the day's over.

'Get a glass of water, and having broken an egg, and separated the white from the yolk, throw the former into it, and place it in the sunshine. You will soon see, with a little aid from your fancy, the ropes and yards of a vessel, if your husband is to be a sailor, or plough and team, if he is to be a farmer.

'Borrow a wedding ring, and suspend it *steadily* in a tall wine-glass by a hair taken from your own head. Think on your sweetheart, if you desire to be assured of his constancy; or on the one you desire for a lover; and if the fates are propitious, the ring will strike against the sides of the glass.

'Get some hemp seed, take it into the garden at midnight, and scattering it, repeat these words, —

Hemp seed I sow, hemp seed I hoe,
In hopes that my true love will come after me and mow.

'You will then see the apparition of your future lover with a scythe, in the act of mowing.

'Get a piece of wedding-cake, and carry it upstairs backwards; tie it in your left stocking, with your right garter, and place it under your pillow. Get into bed backwards, keeping strict silence all the while, and your dreams will reveal to you your predestined sweetheart. These "ceremonies due" must be done aright, or the divination fails.'

It is good to know one old St Ives tradition still flourishes. As has been the custom for many, many years, model boat sailing takes place every Good Friday. Originally the sailing took place on the Crock Bank Pool, a stretch of water which, at low tide, went from Pednolver Point to Smeaton's Pier. Models, including schooners and brigs, luggers and yachts, were built from planks.

In recent years the venue has moved to Consols Pool, Hellesveor, St Ives — close to the junction of the B330 Land's End—St Ives road and the B3311 road: St Ives to Penzance via Nancledra.

Why this little sailing ritual, and why on Good Friday?

Good Friday, for obvious reasons, is both a deeply religious and highly superstitious day. Some farmers never dig, plough or harrow on this sombre date in the calendar; others, in complete contrast, believe that crops will 'come up goody' because of their Good Friday labours.

Maybe the traditional eating of fish on Friday has something to do with it. Personally, though, I think it is a pagan relic, dating back to a time in the distant past when fishermen — always a superstitious breed — would send miniature boats to sea in the expectation that such a gesture would bring safety to their boats.

Another ancient custom belonging to St Ives is Guise Dancing — pronounced 'Geeze'. This was the sport of the twelve days of Christmas. Henry VIII put an embargo on all disguise, but by the 1700s old country customs were recovering again.

St Ives historian Cyril Noall, writing in *The Borough of St Ives 1639-1974,* recalls: 'The young people would dress up in all manner of strange and fancy costumes, and, with their faces covered, visit their friends — and sometimes their enemies — in companies, and dance, and exchange pleasantries in high falsetto voices, hoping to escape recognition. They were usually given a drink and some Christmas fare before proceeding to the next house, where the performance was repeated. The streets at such times wore a carnival aspect, and tradesmen were obliged to shut their shops early on account of the uproar, noise and general lawlessness that prevailed. During the 1920s some well-meaning persons endeavoured to "organise" guise dancing on a more decorous basis; but this proved fatal to a custom which was essentially spontaneous in character.'

Since then, though, Guise Dancing has made an encouraging recovery in the ancient borough. Keith Slocombe, who was an instigator in its resurrection during his Mayoral Year, told me: 'The only concession we have made to the present day is that, because of possible crime, the groups come indoors only at the invitation of the residents. They wear masks or double veils and once they're invited in, they challenge the occupants to guess their true identities; and we've kept up the old tradition which allows the guesser to tell the disguised figure a few home truths without offence being taken.

Royal Customs

In Cornwall we are proud of our Duke of Cornwall.

It must have been a memorable day for the young Prince Charles as he thought back over the exciting glittering events of that historic June day in 1953; the cheering, flag waving crowds along the streets of London, the ornate coach carrying his mother to Westminster, the pageantry, the colour and, above all, that moving moment in the packed Abbey when, alongside his grandmother, he watched the new Queen crowned.

That day that young boy inherited the Dukedom and the Duchy of Cornwall.

Today the Duchy — not the County of Cornwall — covers the estates owned by the Duke in the County as well as those elsewhere, providing 'the heir to the Throne with an opportunity . . . for experience in commerce, experience in industry, in agriculture, in the way of living, and the natures of the people who will one day be his subjects'. His inheritance must surely represent one of the most efficiently run large estates in the world. It stretches across one hundred and forty thousand acres of land. Apart from Duchy of Cornwall properties within this first and last County, the estate extends into Devon, including parts of Dartmoor, Somerset, Dorset, Gloucestershire, Wiltshire, the Isles of Scilly and Kennington with the Oval Cricket Ground, the home of Surrey County Cricket Club.

There are, in fact, some delightfully curious facets surrounding the Duke and Cornwall.

There was, for instance, the Whisky and Soda incident. Whisky and Soda were presented to Prince Charles on Monday 19

◀ Lieutenant-Colonel Molesworth-St Aubyn presenting Whisky and Soda to Prince Charles at Launceston in 1973.

November 1973 when he received his Feudal Dues as Duke of Cornwall during a three-hour visit to Launceston. The ancient ceremony 'in recollection of days long past' was last performed by his grandfather, King George VI in December 1937 — eleven years before Prince Charles was born.

The ceremony, watched by a large crowd containing hundreds of school children, was held in the grounds of the Norman castle. On this occasion Whisky and Soda had no alcoholic content — they were part of a quaint ceremony. They were a pair of greyhounds which formed one of several dues rendered to Prince Charles in the form of rent. The dogs, loaned by Mr and Mrs Ralph Parsons of Egloshayle, Wadebridge, were presented by Lieutenant-Colonel John Arscott Molesworth-St Aubyn. The Bailiff and Town Clerk read a proclamation, reciting details of ancient tenure in sergeanty. He stated that the Manor of Cabillia was held by the service of paying to the Duke one grey cloak as often as he should pass through Cornwall. The cloak on this occasion was provided by Viscount Clifden, then aged eighty-six, who was brought to the ceremony in a wheelchair. Among the rents offered in token 'in recollection of days long past' were a pair of gilt spurs, one pound of cummin, a salmon spear, one carriage of wood, a goatskin, a pair of white gloves, one hundred predecimilisation shillings, one pound of pepper from the Borough of Launceston, and a bow d'Auburne presented by the Mayor of Truro.

Having given each a white rod, Prince Charles said: 'I hereby confirm you and those you represent, tenants, and give you and them peacable and quiet seizin and possession of the Manors, Lands and tenancies which you hold or represent according to ancient custom.'

Lieutenant-Colonel Molesworth-St Aubyn still affectionately remembers those two greyhounds, Whisky and Soda. 'They towed me down the road to the Castle and at that point I needed all my strength to hold on to them. Apart from that and treading all over my shoes, they were very well behaved. When the Prince arrived we were called in turn. The Prince was absolutely charming and couldn't have been nicer. As I put the leash into his hands, he said, "I know I'm not allowed to keep them." To which I replied, "I'm very glad to hear that, Sir." The reason behind this conversation was that when my father presented greyhounds to King George VI, he asked my father "What will you do if I keep them". So when Jock

Stanier, the Duchy Land Steward at that time, asked me to take part in the ceremony, I said, "Yes, I'll do it, but I'm not going to risk that embarrassment, so will you please make it quite clear that the greyhounds don't belong to me." '

Hopefully, one day, Prince William, in his role as Duke of Cornwall, will be here receiving another pair of symbolic greyhounds thereby perpetuating this old Royal custom.

Moreover, unless ancient tradition is changed, Prince William, like his father and previous Dukes of Cornwall, will be entitled to 'Royal Fish' but that's a dubious privilege in that these include any whales washed up on Cornish beaches.

Whale and sturgeon are both rated 'Royal fish' because of their superior intelligence. When caught near the coast or thrown ashore they become the property of the Crown. Porpoises are also considered Royal fish. It has been said by ancient writers that in the case of a whale, it is to be divided between the king and the queen: the head being the king's and the tail the queen's. As far as the Duchy of Cornwall is concerned though, Royal fish belong to Prince Charles. But if carcasses of whales are washed up on Duchy shores, they have to be returned to the sea and destroyed at the expense of the Duchy.

There are, however, some intriguing bonuses for the Duke of Cornwall. He is entitled to treasure trove and *Bona Vacantia:* the estates of people who die intestate without any known next-of-kin.

And, of course, if Prince William develops a passion for golf, he has a delightful facility here in Cornwall in the St Enodoc golf course. 6,069 feet long and of championship standard, St Enodoc is a Duchy of Cornwall property. All in all, then, some of the traditions of our Duke of Cornwall and the Duchy deserve inclusion in our catalogue, decidedly curious but still cherished by many who remain loyally Royalist.

THE FAMOUS OLD
Punch Bowl Inn
AND STABLE RESTAURANT
Worthington
'E'
BOWL INN
FREE HOUSE
AA

Some Cornish Inns

The inn, like the church, has become an integral part of our history and landscape, and here in Cornwall we are blessed with some really beautiful inns — some too with curious features. Any exploration among the curiosities of Cornwall naturally draws the traveller to them.

The Punch Bowl at Lanreath is one of the loveliest, most interesting inns in all Cornwall, and it has a most intriguing feature. Anyone looking for a bar at the Punch Bowl will be disappointed. There are none! This is one of the last inns in Britain which prefers to use the old-fashioned term 'kitchen'. In more than four hundred years, the Punch Bowl has been used as a court house, coaching inn and smugglers' distribution centre: a varied career to say the least. It has a fine wrought iron sign by the distinguished painter Augustus John.

Edna Oxley, a former owner of the inn, told me a fascinating legend linking the Punch Bowl and the church across the road. 'Long, long ago,' she said, 'Lanreath had a very old rector who married a very young and very beautiful wife. The rector, though, was finding the parish a bit too much for him. . . and he acquired the services of a curate, a very charming young man. The inevitable happened. The curate and the rector's wife fell in love. Everybody in the village knew about the affair . . . that is, everybody except the rector. And, in his ignorance, the rector invited the curate to dinner on Christmas Day, but before the meal he suggested the two of them should go down into the cellar to get a bottle of wine; going down into the cellar the old man tripped and fell, and, as a result of

◀'The Punchbowl at Lanreath has a fine sign painted by Augustus John.'

the fall, died. Some of the villagers were suspicious about the rector's end, but they kept quiet. The funeral took place and the rector was laid to rest, and in time the curate became the rector and married the young widow.

'But that wasn't the end of the old rector. He came back in the shape of a very black and very scurrilous cockerel and began haunting the rectory, tormenting the villagers, and the young lovers in particular. He was a very wily cockerel . . . nobody succeeded in catching him. . . a group of local men, armed with pitch forks, cornered him in a barn, but again the cockerel was too wily for them. He flew over their heads and out of the barn, but he made the mistake of flying through an open window of the Punch Bowl. It so happened that the landlady was just taking some bread out of the oven, and with great presence of mind she slammed the door as he flew in, which was the end of the cockerel and the old rector.'

Ye Olde Punch Bowl & Ladle Inn at Penelewey — claims to be the only inn with that name.

Not to be confused with this inn is another splendid Cornish hostelry. Ye Olde Punch Bowl & Ladle at Penelewey near Feock further down the county. Interestingly Ye Olde Punch Bowl and Ladle claims to be the only inn with that name in the kingdom. Some have said this is an eleventh-century inn which would make it the oldest inn in England, but alas there is no documentary evidence. Despite that shortcoming it remains a beautiful old inn with elaborate thatch and inside its four walls there is a strong aura of the past, intensified by the dark doorways and the old oak beams. There is, too, a large fireplace with an odd chimney. This is called the 'Bosun's Pipe' where theoretically smuggled tobacco should have gone up in smoke under the supervision of the Revenue Men. One just wonders how much went up in such smoke — and how much was enjoyed illegally.

Still on the subject of rare names: who would expect to find an hostelry called The Norway Inn here in Cornwall?

But you will do just that at Perranarworthal, on the road linking Truro and Falmouth, and you will find the reason for this foreign name in Cornish history. Long ago, when the River Fal was more navigable than it is now, Norwegian vessels, trading with Cornwall, unloaded their cargoes at a quay not far away. Business was a two-way thing in that they brought in timber, often in the shape of pit props, and took away tin from the Cornish mines.

The inn in those days was an important centre for traders, and not all the overseas callers spoke English; consequently the landlord insisted on his staff speaking several languages, especially Norwegian. Happily that tradition continues to this day.

Zennor contains some of the loveliest acres in all Cornwall, and the Tinners Arms happens to be one of my favourite inns. D. H. Lawrence, who lived nearby for part of the 1914-18 War, was a customer here — but not a popular one. Over a pint he was inclined to speak out against the war, and did nothing to conceal his loathing of the Lloyd George government. Worst of all, he and his wife Frieda, the daughter of a Prussian Baron, sang German songs loudly and defiantly.

In August 1917 a German submarine was sighted off the coast near Zennor. Destroyers and planes hurried to the spot, and a slick of black oil on the water appeared, showing that one charge, at least, had found its target. Allegations grew — lights signalling out to sea at night — and one day Frieda was halted by a coastguard, who

Left: D.H. Lawrence and Frieda his wife. 'He was a customer at The Tinners Arms at Zennor (below) but not a popular one.'

feeling her rucksack declared: 'Ah, a camera!' Frieda instead produced a loaf of bread, but gossip and suspicion were spreading.

The Lawrences' mail was withheld and scrutinised. Later soldiers searched the cottage in their absence and finally a posse appeared, consisting of a young Army officer, the friendly local policeman and two detectives. The contents of every cupboard and drawer were examined and a notebook of Lawrence's concerning his Nottingham days was confiscated. The young officer set seal on the visit by presenting an expulsion order: the Lawrences were to leave Cornwall within three days and without explanation.

'And that's what you call English justice!' hissed Frieda.

It was — and in 1917 it was Cornish justice too.

A more recent customer of note at The Tinners Arms was Lord Hunt of Everest fame. The cliffs hereabouts were used for climbing — the schooling ground of mountaineers.

But the curiosity of the inn lies in its name. Tin mining was once a vast industry; yet incredibly I'm told this is the *only* Tinners Arms in the whole of Britain.

The name, in fact, dates from the days when the mines of Penwith were living things — today only Geevor functions in this part of Cornwall. Mining company board meetings were held upstairs at The Tinners, with drinks and dinner following the business discussions. So when you drink and eat here you are part of an old Cornish tradition, and either side of your visit to the inn, take time to explore this bit of Cornwall. The land and seascapes are among the most memorable anywhere in Britain.

From Zennor the coastal road down into St Ives is one of the great joys of Penwith. Words cannot convey the grandeur of moor, cliffs, sea and sky. Down in the town is one of the real character waterfront inns: The Sloop.

The inns of Penwith for many years had their own special Poet Laureate in the person of Arthur Caddick, who lived in a cottage called Windswept at Nancledra. I always think of Arthur and The Sloop with affection because one of our very first Bossiney titles was a book of comic verses by Arthur Caddick, entitled *Broadsides from Bohemia*, 'In Praise of Painters, Publicans and other Cornish Saints'. Moreover the book opened with a poem called Top Person Talking:

Put out my pink plastic bow, dear,
And wipe out those splashes of soup,
And spray me with Gentleman's Eau, dear,
I wish to take wine at the Sloop.

The patrons are utterly tops, dear,
All Mayfair plonked down in the west,
Not tradesmen who keep little shops, dear,
Just Debrett and Who's Who and the Best.

> *'By Gad! How it heartens a fella,*
> *To find finger-bowls out on the bar,*
> *And a pedigree cat in the cellar,*
> *And C.D. on the cellarman's car!*

You'd like to trot down for a drink, dear,
Alright then, but wash both your feet,
And sling on that bra trimmed with Mink, dear,
You never know who you may meet.

The aristocrats down at the Sloop, dear,
Would never wear anything brash,
They jump through an autocrat's hoop, dear,
Like gentry at Bath under Nash.

> *'By Gad! This will shake the Tregenna!*
> *I bet British Railways will droop,*
> *And, darling, please lend me a tenner —*
> *They're always so flush at the Sloop.'*

It was a slim volume, but it helped to put Bossiney on the regional publishing map; it gave a lot of pleasure and fired one perceptive reviewer to write: 'He brings the broadside and the barb of humour to a dull-grey society of vanity and pomposity. He wears the jester's motley and the sage's gown.'

Arthur, who wrote *One Hundred Doors Are Open*, a guide to Cornish inns in the 1950's, was the first writer I really met — until one evening in a St Ives bar, writers had always been 'personalities' viewed from a distance. I can still see him on that summer Friday evening: tall and wearing a red bow tie. There was the hint of the Shakespearean actor about him and I was half afraid to speak to him as his rich voice sent wit and merriment around that smoke-filled room. Pints and poems flowed, and from that evening I was hooked on authors.

Inn signs are a fascinating subject. One of the most puzzling is to be found near Delabole. When Leo and Joyce Henderson transformed an aged farmhouse into a slate-hung freehouse, they chose the Poldark Inn as the name: a shrewd choice. It's extraordinary to think nobody had hit upon the idea before because, thanks to Winston Graham's brilliant Poldark novels and the huge success of the BBC TV series based on these novels, Cornwall will for ever be the land of Poldark. But when Leo Henderson's brother painted the sign outside the inn, he somehow mixed his Poldark characters, and instead of Ross Poldark, in the person of actor Robin Ellis, looking down on the patrons, it happens to be the face of his arch enemy George Warleggan, as portrayed by Ralph Bates on the TV screen.

Robin Ellis, who wrote a very good book on the series for Bossiney, was highly amused when I told him of the mistaken identity. 'Typical,' said "Ross Poldark", 'Warleggan getting in on the act!'

On this tour of Cornish inns, we are now back in North Cornwall.

Boscastle remains a gem: one of North Cornwall's most attractive villages set on a dramatic coastline and flanked by some beautiful countryside. The cottages at Boscastle are among the most picturesque in the whole county.

Once though it must have had quite a hard drinking reputation. There was a time when this small village boasted as many as eighteen ale houses. Today there are just three full licences.

Many visitors to Boscastle must look at the Cobweb Inn and wonder 'Why Cobweb?' The answer is simple. When the inn acquired a full licence back in 1945 one room was festooned with cobwebs, generations of them. So the name was a natural.

The building, dating from the late 1600s, was formerly a warehouse and office. The interesting thing about the cobwebs is they had been deliberately retained. In earlier times when the merchants housed their wines and spirits in this section of the building, they firmly believed the cobwebs helped to keep the flies away from the casks — and anyone removing them was fired!

Unfortunately the cobwebs have declined in recent years. Landlord Ivor Bright told me they had become heavy and stringy due to the atmosphere. The cobwebs may be only a fraction of their former scale, but The Cobweb remains a friendly inn and inside

COBWEB INN
RESTAURANT
The
Cobweb
Inn
free house
Restaurant
KKJ 889L

there is one espescially interesting object: a finely carved figure-head. It came from *The Welm*, a Swedish ship that perished in a wicked gale on Black Rock, a few miles up the coast near Crackington Haven, around 1890. Despite valiant rescue attempts, only one member of the crew — the mate — survived.

Any itinerary of Cornwall's inns really ought to include a haunted property. One of my favourites is The Bush Inn at Morwenstow. In November 1968 disaster struck here when a fire destroyed the entire thatched roof and half the ancient building. At the height of the fire some people claimed to have seen a dark shadowy figure moving away from the blazing inn. The interesting fact is prior to that fire The Bush had a considerable haunted reputation. Back in 1979 when I interviewed landlord Jim Gregory for *Occult In The West,* he told me of substantial evidence that had built up over the years relating to ghostly sounds and positive sightings. But intriguingly since the fire, Jim admits he has not seen or heard anything which defies human explanation. 'It's fair to say other people claim to have seen the figure of a man inside the inn since 1968 and I don't disbelieve them, but personally I've experienced nothing of a Supernatural nature in recent years. Maybe the fire did exorcise something.'

Fire, of course, is one of the four elemental forces, and has long been regarded by students of the Supernatural as a powerful agent for purification and renewal. So perhaps the fire, a terrible disaster at the time, did change more than the physical character of The Bush. 'But happily it was always a benign spirit,' reflected Jim Gregory. Whether you are a cynic or a believer in Supernatural possibility, I recommend a visit to The Bush on any tour of Hawker Country. It remains a warm friendly place — and an area of serious speculation.

◀The Cobweb Inn at Boscastle: '. . . one room was festooned with cobwebs, generations of them.'

Religious Curiosities

Gwennap Pit is more than a Cornish curiosity. It is a great gathering-place of Methodist people in Cornwall. They first gathered here on Whit Monday 1807 and have done so every calendar since — not even Hitler's War years stopped them.

But this grassy amphitheatre is a puzzle. Some believe Gwennap Pit may be the sunken floor of a filled-up mine; a distinct possibility because it stands in the heart of old mining country. It has outstanding acoustics, and Arthur Mee was moved to call it 'Cornwall's Albert Hall, over three hundred yards round with grassy tiers and seats'. David Mudd, in his *Cornwall and Scilly Peculiar* wrote: 'An annual application of grass and stone can have as stirring an effect in rejuvenating the Christian batteries of a Cornishman as a dash of distilled water in the batteries of the car he drives. There can be no doubt that the atmosphere of super-charged faith that annually pervades Gwennap Pit is as strong now as in the days when the Wesleys came to Cornwall. It stands, or rather is sunk, a stone's throw from Carharrack and St Day, an unbelievably orderly natural amphitheatre of grass and stone.'

The great John Wesley preached here on several occasions. On one visit he recorded: 'I think this is the most magnificent spectacle which is to be seen this side of heaven . . .' By Wesley's reckoning as many as 25,000 Cornish people gathered here for one of his sermons.

In Cornwall you cannot escape John Wesley and you cannot begin to understand Cornwall without reference to him. Wesley's sheer physical achievements were enormous. He rode over 250,000 miles, sometimes covering 70 miles and delivering three sermons in the same day — initially many of them before hostile gatherings. Even here in Cornwall, he had eggs and stones thrown at him. He wrote 233 original works, including a four volume history of England, earning £40,000 in royalties and giving every penny away.

Outside and beyond all this, he set up a free medical dispensary, adapted an electrical machine for healing, opened spinning and knitting shops for the poor, and not only founded the Kingswood School for boys but wrote the text books as well.

Cornwall is peppered with Methodist Chapels, reminders of Wesley's fiery message and its impact. Some time back I was in the chapel at Lanivet, which is now a fish and chip shop; it was a strange experience because in the high noon of Methodism that building, and hundreds more, rang with 'Alleluyas'. Sadly congregations in many places have shrunk, and some chapels have closed. Yet the spirit of Wesley is still alive; attend a Harvest Festival or a Chapel Anniversary in one of the better supported chapels and the feeling is he may be gone but he is not forgotten — nor his brother Charles, for the Cornish, like the Welsh, love a good hymn or song.

Derek Parker, a Cornishman who trained as a young journalist on *The Cornishman* newspaper at Penzance, in his book *The Westcountry,* had one splendid story relating to a St Ives chapel:

The stone at Zennor from which Wesley preached.

'. . . there are still some delightfully original local preachers,' he wrote in the early 1970s, 'though perhaps few likely to give out the exasperated complaint of one old man . . . A drought had ended, and the wind and the rain were beating on the chapel roof and beating down (he knew) the crops also. "O Lord," he prayed, "truly we have had a long spell of it, and constantly have we offered petitions for rain for the cisterns and the crops; but, O Lord, *this is ridiculous!*" '

Another preacher in the county prefaced a prayer with the words: 'Looard, as thou wilt ha' seen in this week's *West Briton* . . .'

Now a presentday churchgoer or reader may think these are *only* good stories, but even in my lifetime I can think of some incredible characters who preached from our chapel pulpits. As recently as the 1950s, I can recall one forthright preacher who, in condemning the then modern trends, paused in mid-sermon and turning to some young girls in the choir stalls, said 'and as for you, painted Jezebelles!'

Cornwall, as I said earlier, is essentially Non-Conformist.

And nobody personified that spirit better than Billy Bray. After

The Quaker Meeting House at Come-to-Good has existed since 1710.

Wesley came a whole regiment of Non-Conformist preachers and Billy must have inspired many of them. A Cornish tin miner, he thought nothing of working six days underground and then on the seventh, 'The Lord's Day', walking twenty miles to preach. Born at Twelveheads in the year 1794, he was a pioneering spirit of the Bible Christian Methodists, and is reputed to have built a small chapel with his own hands. Three chapels were all closely linked with Billy Bray and all remain — though the chapel at Carharrack is now a farm building.

My great-aunt, Mabel Williams, of St Austell, one of A.L. Rowse's first teachers, told me how a great-great somebody of mine — someone a good few generations back — was listening to Billy Bray one Sunday evening, proclaiming on the need for faith in God. 'I haven't a good overcoat for the winter,' Billy declared from the pulpit, 'but I put my trust in the Lord.' After the service was over, my ancestor went and handed over his Sunday best overcoat: a gift for the visiting preacher. Billy Bray was wearing it on his next visit to the chapel some months later. 'The Lord hath provided . . .' he told his congregation.

One of the most beautiful religious buildings is at Come-to-Good: a name in itself that deserves a place in any catalogue of Cornish Curiosities.

It lies in a hollow at the foot of a steep hill. 'Certainly it is good to come to,' reflected Arthur Mee as he journeyed through Cornwall in the 1930s. Come-to-Good has existed since 1710 as a Quaker Meeting House, which makes it one of the oldest in the country. It was originally a plain rectangular building of whitewashed cob with a thatched roof, and cost £68.18s.3d to construct. The loft was added in 1717, but the porch, children's room and kitchen were built in 1967.

Come-to-Good was once Cwm-ty-coit, meaning 'the coombe by the dwelling in the wood'. Although it now seems isolated, when it was built it lay on one of the main routes from Truro to Falmouth. George Fox, who formed the Religious Society of Friends from the 'seekers' of the time, visited Cornwall in 1656, when he had the misfortune to end up in Launceston Gaol: the result of the current Quaker persecution. Early Quaker meetings were held in a farmhouse, and many people were fined and imprisoned, until the Toleration Act of 1689. The first meeting at Come-to-Good was on 13 June 1710. 'Public Friends there were Thomas Gwinn, Thomas

Giddy, John Taylor (Marazion), James Hoskyn and Mary Scantlebury.'

At one time there is a record of a thousand people attending, when an overflow meeting had to be held outside. In 1755 the lease for Come-to-Good was granted to one William Phillips by William Lemon, for one thousand years at an annual rent of one shilling. The lease cost £52.10s. Since then it has been assigned by Trust Deeds to the Friends, who still meet here on Sunday afternoons.

The Church of England too has a curiosity. Temple is — or more accurately was — a religious curiosity.

It was once the Cornish Gretna Green. After the Reformation, this tiny Moorland church remained outside the authority of the Bishop — until 1774 anyway — and Carew was moved to record that: 'Many a bad marriage bargain is there yearly slubbered up.'

Temple's history started to take some significant shape in the twelfth century when the Knights Templar built a hospice here for travellers. Eight hundred years ago it must have been a desolate place. I came here on a winter's morning and sat alone in the tiny church — there are just twenty chairs with built-in kneelers. You could hear the silence, and in that peaceful place I thought of poor Edith Gilpin of Temple, who in 1777 gave birth to an illegitimate child and was forced, barefooted and bareheaded, to make a public confession of her 'sin' at morning services in Blisland and Cardinham churches.

◄Temple Church: '. . . once the Cornish Gretna Green.'

ALSO AVAILABLE

CURIOSITIES OF DEVON

by Michael Williams. A catalogue of Curiosities in Devon: curious characters, curious customs, strange architecture — an absorbing exploration of some of the County's unusual features.

STRANGE STORIES FROM DEVON

by Rosemary Anne Lauder and Michael Williams. 46 photographs.
Strange shapes and places — strange characters — the man they couldn't hang, and a Salcombe mystery, the Lynmouth disaster and a mysterious house are only some of the strange stories.

'A riveting read'. The Plymouth Times

'. . . well-written and carefully edited'

Monica Wyatt, Teignmouth Post & Gazette

CORNISH MYSTERIES

by Michael Williams. 40 photographs.
Cornish Mysteries is a kind of jig-saw puzzle in words and pictures. The power of charming, mysterious shapes in the Cornish landscape, the baffling murder case of Mrs Hearn are just some fascinating ingredients.

'. . . superstitions, dreams, murder, Lyonesse, the legendary visit of the boy Jesus to Cornwall, and much else. Splendid, and sometimes eerie, chapters.'

The Methodist Recorder

SUPERNATURAL IN CORNWALL

by Michael Williams. 24 photographs.

'. . . a book of fact, not fiction . . . covers not only apparitions and things that go bump in the night, but also witchcraft, clairvoyancy, spiritual healing, even wart charming . . .' Jenny Myerscough on BBC

'Serious students of ghost-hunting will find a fund of locations.'

Graham Danton on Westward TV

SUPERSTITION AND FOLKLORE

by Michael Williams. 45 photographs.
Romany reflections, old country customs, interviews with superstitious people, folklore from both Devon and Cornwall, omens and coincidences are all featured.

'. . . has all the ingredients of a mini bestseller.' Cornwall Courier

STRANGE HAPPENINGS IN CORNWALL

by Michael Williams. 35 photographs. Strange shapes and strange characters; healing and life after death; reincarnation and Spiritualism; murders and mysteries are only some of the contents in this fascinating book.

'. . . this eerie Cornish collection.' David Foot, Western Daily Press